SALVAE

#11
ALREADY, NOT YET

AUTUMN / WINTER 2021

Contents

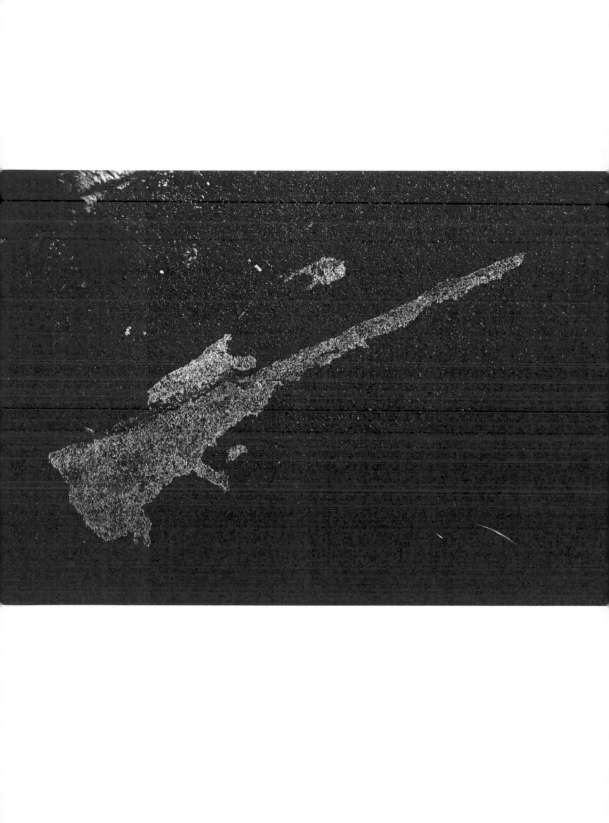

HEBA HAYEK

Did You Know?

When the morning bell rang, hundreds of students from Years One to Six would rush into the school court*. Each class lined up in a perfect row, together forming a U-shape facing the stage. There the principal stood to start the day and star students led the half-hour-long morning assembly. The daily routine involved the scouts hoisting the flag for the national anthem, followed by a light exercise, a beautifully recited Qur'an verse, *Did You Know?* fun facts and a poem at the end. I was usually the poem girl.

Wednesday was Year One's day to lead the routine, so my classmates and I prepared what we thought was an exquisite schedule in the hope of finally winning the school broadcast badge. Year Four had beaten us to it for three consecutive weeks. That particular morning smelled of ash and pine trees, recalling the forest green of our dutifully worn school uniforms with white embroidered collars.

We were about to share very well-researched historical fun facts when the principal interrupted our schedule for an urgent

---

* With thanks to Hajar Press for their permission to publish extracts from *Sambac Beneath Unlikely Skies*.

9

announcement.

'Ariel Sharon entered the site of Al-Aqsa Mosque today,' she informed us. All the teachers were shaking their heads, murmuring in frustration and disapproval. A scout student from Year Six led a chant, and we all repeated it in unison.

Thawra, thawra, 'a al-mohtal, gheir al-horyeh, ma fi hal!

Revolution against the occupation, we won't accept less than liberation!

'We don't know what will happen, but there are talks of riots and protests. Our duty is to support our nation and protect Jerusalem no matter what, so we will discontinue our morning routine for a collective prayer,' the principal continued.

I stood there in my tiny self with my poem hanging from my pocket, entirely upset with Sharon. We would have to wait another week to win the badge.

I raised my hands, my small palms facing me, fingers covered in faded paint as we prayed for a free Palestine. I wasn't so young that I didn't realise my home had been stolen. After all, as a child of 1994, I had been reared on lullabies protesting the Oslo Agreement and singing for national liberation.

Ahla bunouta bt'oul, al-hokm al-zati mish ma'boul, bidna ntaharrar 'ala toul, min al-zulm wal-este'mar...

And the beautiful girl says, Palestinian autonomy is not enough, we want total liberation from oppression and colonialism...

But I just wanted to read my poem.

The next day, I sat on the eighth-floor balcony at Khalto Mihaela's flat and watched the explosions and smoke all around the city. The Second Intifada had officially been announced, and Mama had to go and pick up my siblings and Mihaela's kids early from school. My classes were in the afternoon, so I hadn't gone to school yet.

Khalto Mihaela made me clătite for the first time that day, a cigarette in one hand and an electric whisk in the other, while news broadcasts blasted through the building's windows.

'Did you know that the Anglo-Zanzibar War of 1896 is considered to be the shortest war in history, lasting for a grand total of thirty-eight minutes?' I said, my mouth full of crepes, powdered sugar smearing everywhere.

'Yes, and we are already three hours into the Second Intifada,' she said in her Romanian accent.

'Did you know that—'

'No more, eat your food or I take it.'

She had just unmuted the TV for the afternoon briefing when the presenter announced that there was breaking news. Khalto Mihaela didn't understand Standard Arabic, so we usually translated for her in spoken Arabic whenever she was listening to important stories.

On the screen, footage streamed of a father trying to shield his son, as bullets rained down on them both.

'What are they saying?' She looked at me, a little unsure whether she really wanted me to translate.

I'm not sure I even understood what was being said myself. I was six, and I had just seen a child getting murdered on TV as his father tried to protect him from Israeli snipers. The presenter was loud and angry. We were both upset and scared.

Mihaela gave me a hug, and more clătite.

'You know, Allah will never forget this. This is our land, and no one can take it from us.'

'It's not your land, Khalto.'

'I've lived here for five times your age, kid. It is my home now. Romania is my home too.'

I wondered how one could have two homes. I was six and barely able to have one.

Mihaela turned off the TV and let me read her the poem I was supposed to read at our school assembly, a small way to compensate for what I had just witnessed.

That day, smeared with sugar and fear, my body comprehended the first signs of the desire for justice and revenge. I read a poem about sunrise, holding the image in my mind of Muhammad al-Durrah, riddled with bullets in his father's lap.

BARNABY RAINE

Left Fukuyamaism: Politics in Tragic Times

In 1991, a documentary crew witnessed the dissolution of the Communist Party of Great Britain*.

'The End of the Party' shows us three demographics. The young(er) Eurocommunists of the Party leadership have the chic graphics and the hard truths; confidently they berate an ageing audience to accept that 'the era of Communist Parties is over' as they push for a name change. When they win, the few students in the room cheer and rise to their feet in applause. They want to be part of the future, not just the past. Rose Kerrigan stays sitting. Born in 1903 to Jewish immigrants from the Russian empire, Rose tells us how she lost her first job in 1917 for defending a conscientious objector during the First World War. She shows us the tea sets and the Gorky novels she brought back from stays in the new Russia in the 1930s. Those trips were her recovery of the land her parents left

* With deep thanks to David Camfield, without whom this article would have been impossible, and Charlotte Heltai, without whom it would have been worse. I am grateful, constantly, to Jonas Marvin for encouraging me. The mistakes are all my own.

and the winning of a land they never had. Becoming a Communist was her social mobility, her entry into broader and richer life-worlds. But it came with community, and with love and loyalty for her roots, and so without the particular sort of trampling on others that the term social mobility more often suggests. Her husband fought in Spain, then raised money everywhere and against the odds to push back fascism there. She knows that people want her to apologise now for being a Communist, but they always have – since the days of the trenches. She believes that every human being everywhere should be treated equally, she tells us, without all the hierarchies of race and nation and gender and class to which most outside her militant minority doff their caps. Her new Party leaders find her an embarrassment. They talk of the need for reinvention, they know the Communists have become a relic. After their win at the conference, the new project faded quickly until, seeking ever broader and shallower alliances, they delivered Moscow's gold to an insipid campaign for electoral reform.

There is sorrow and beauty in watching Rose. She lives still in the hopes of Red Clydeside, Glasgow's destroyed working class radicalism. She remembers visiting the first supermarket in the Soviet Union. She doesn't tell us that everything was perfect there, or even easy. But she came from tenements, looked up at Soviet skyscrapers, and thought of all the cynics for whom a world without suffering was impossible. She hoped that one day soon the Russians would prove them wrong. The shipyards of Glasgow, with kinder cultures of solidarity than the bosses preach, might be with them then. It would be possible for others – for her friends and family – to believe at last. She remembers not a naïvely glorified past, but a real one: real pain but also a trajectory, a future she is told now to consign to the past. She stays in this memory because it is possible there, and so hard outside it, to root the dedication to a better world in something concrete.

Rose gets off the train and shuffles into the conference hall to register her protest against the end of Communism with a capital-C. She walks past a small band of young things in black leather jackets. 'No matter how you change your name', they shout into the hall, 'you still play the bosses' game!' These are the savvy twins to the Eurocommunist reformers, the young Stalinists who know which way the wind is blowing. They've left the Party, and they call it a corpse. Their newspaper is the *Leninist*, and against the stream they champion (albeit critically) the Russian tanks that once rolled into Budapest and Prague. Theirs is no mass party. They are the enlightened few. To them, as to the Eurocommunists, Rose who will not give up her old Party is an old fool.

Rose died in 1995. The *Leninist* is now the *Weekly Worker*, and its writers are ageing too. They have moved on from their Stalinism. But there is a new if modest proliferation of radicals now who would have baffled 1990s commentators; young people in Europe and North America who want to sound like the old Communists. On podcasts and on social media, in political parties and in unions, they salute authoritarian state power past and present. They speak, they say, in the name of socialism. They amass thousands of followers online. They are not the dwindling band of pensioners who remember subsidised cruises on the Volga. They don an aesthetic of kitsch cheek or unsentimental realism or, somehow, both. The small Communist Party of Britain (founded by some of the old CPGB's anti-Eurocommunists) feels the need to issue slightly embarrassed social media guidelines for its younger members, opposing glorification of Stalin. In the resurgent and newly youthful Democratic Socialists of America, veering since 2016 from the margins of the political margins to their foreground, critics of 'campist' admiration for ostensibly anti-US bureaucrats overseas find themselves isolated and then booted off the International Committee. In New York, a much-billed conference on 'China and the Left' spills over with enthusiasm for the Chinese state. In Britain, the Corbynites at Novara Media cover protests in Havana by insisting 'that violent disorder will be punished through the legal system.'

Are these the heirs of Rose Kerrigan? Some of the new

campists seem to reflect the hecklers outside the conference hall in 1991 more than anyone inside it: loud and confident, committed to Five Year Plans in part for the shock value, and detached from most mass politics. Though Rose spoke with melancholy of the disappointments of the Soviet Union, some in this band have the deepest suspicion for anything but adulation for a project that was not theirs. They never knew its heyday. But they want Rose's world. They certainly do not regard her with haughty contempt. One of their sympathetic features is their protest against a left in search of a future that would denigrate its past as nothing but awkward.

'Campism' originally meant support for a mighty 'socialist camp' stretching without interruption from Berlin to Beijing. Campists supported workers on strike against pay cuts and humiliations in Detroit but not in Poland, where everything was flipped; dissident workers there could only further the interests of global capital and the CIA, in the campist view, and their bosses better represented the international working class. Now that camp is gone, but campism is back. It can name the defence or the admiration (not the same thing) of states past, present or both. It can be the garb for the hardest sectarianism or the softest opportunism. It can think its camp headquarters were once in Moscow or Algiers or that they remain in Beijing or in Caracas. The unifying connection is a hard-nosed scorn for hypocritical imperialists and leftwing idealists alike who rush to denounce gulags. Campism today names a common turn within several different parts of the left, rather than a single current. Why is this happening now? What mood does it express? The critique of ideology, asking what the emergence of particular forms of thought might reveal about their epoch, is in need of renewal. Treating thought and feeling together might be one way of renewing it.

In Vivian Gornick's classic *Romance of American Communism* (and in the moving 1983 documentary, 'Seeing Red', on American Communists recruited in the 1930s) the following point is already half-visible. The affective dimensions of contemporary campism are rooted in love: the forbidden romance, the wistful longing for the departed, and the privately desolate love that *settles for less*.

Our aim, like Marx's, should be a form of critique capable of grasping the conditions in which a given idea feels plausible. That is rare enough on the left today, where denunciation can be more pleasurable. And though Marxist orthodoxy hews to the rational reconstruction of objective interests as Marx's great power – now deployed to tell people they are proletarian even, or especially, when they think otherwise – in fact Marx's work is imbued with sensitivity to the feeling of the world, to its emotional experience, as central in the genesis of political activity. As a young man in Paris, he named not one kind of alienation but two: the objective process by which our labour and its products come to dominate us, and also its subjective corollary where the worker 'does not feel at home' in work. By the writing of *Capital* twenty years later, the modern factory had become a key site in the construction of the revolutionary subject – though more wage-labourers then toiled on farms and in domestic service than in England's industrial workshops – in part because the concentration of workers there introduced a novel experience, where 'the labourer co-operates systematically with others', and so feels the world of production for the first time as a site pregnant with the possibility of social management. There is a challenge here to us, to think of affects not only as the property of our irrational opponents but as the phenomena we need too for politics.

First, though, we would do well to understand jealously how structures of feeling now predominant sustain politics other than those we would choose. The question here is both fundamental and general, though this current offers only one window onto it. The question is: what kinds of politics of antagonism and hope flourish, after the End of History?

The Wistful Past
There is today a romance of the illicit amid the failure of the accepted. This much is obvious. People sometimes have damaging affairs when all is not well in their stable and boring relationships. They

crave the liberating rush of setting aside their better judgement, which feels merely oppressive once it stops feeling like a route to their flourishing. The 'alt-right', so-called, provides a similar kind of outlet after decades of stagnation and disappointment from the established order. If that order with its gods – 'liberalism', 'democracy' – is predicated on a rejection of Nazism and Stalinism, then the most shocking thing anyone can do is to embrace either label enthusiastically. And why not, if faced with rising rents and insecure employment and the uselessness of those gods? It is of course important that enough time has elapsed after their defeat for these demons to feel like myths spun by the ruling class, losing their reality; part of the irony ought to be that Stalinism was really very *grey*, so it takes fading memories for it to be constructed as risqué. This is a story of forbidden love.

If the major brand of youth radicalism in the global North today involves the suffocating moralism of Mark Fisher's 'vampire castle', here is a language for resenting power without the masochism and the atomistic paranoias of contemporary identity pessimism: how refreshing to switch a fragile and frightened 'safe space' for all the might and pride of a marching band in Red Square. There is an important affective dimension to all of this, just as Trump without the lurid vulgarity – a Trump entirely serious – would not have had quite the same popular pull. Shock value is almost all we have in pessimistic times, where social transformation to overthrow the world's rulers might be impossible but horrifying them and making them uncomfortable offers some escape.

That brings us to the ubiquity of nostalgia as a form of politics today. The right has lost its 1980s vanguard optimism: no longer 'Morning in America' but 'American Carnage', instead. Its battle-cry now is not the making of a new world of flexible markets but the rescue of a past order trashed by multiculturalism and feminism and much else besides. Social democracy also speaks in an overwhelmingly nostalgic key, longing for the post-war golden age destroyed by neoliberal conspiracy in the 1980s. Right and left, then, are united in this basic language. Climate change and automation feature as harbingers of coming doom across the political spectrum. Even centrist technocratic crisis-fighters see little in the way of an exhilarating future. For political hope, for sunny days and lost innocence, the norm now is to look to the past. Make America Great *Again*. Take *Back* Control. One must choose a past to venerate, and so people rushing to the left are called on to find a past of their own: the longer-lasting the better, so that its endurance can act as a smack in the face to all of hegemony's doubts about whether anything different is possible at all.

For some, who lack much political activity outside Twitter or who join tiny grouplets, the comforts of the past are an alibi for the barrenness of the present; in this The New Stalinists, who at least want to have fun in *the joy of the provocative*, are just more self-aware than the rest of the left which often plays the same sentimental game but takes itself more seriously. We cosplay and say, 'Another World Was Possible'. Often though, the shock value attained by Cold War nostalgia satisfies urges for radicalism in a pessimistic moment, while the real nostalgia remains for social democracy. Internet Stalinisms and campisms in the global North are diverse, but in recent years some have come from the most enthusiastic supporters of more mainstream electoral lefts.

It makes sense to combine these two forms of longing. To speak sentimentally of the USSR is not only to summon memories of a world where the word 'socialism' seemed to mean something mighty and frightening to power. It is also to remember a time when the very language of 'class' and its politics had firmer, apparently easier, industrial foundations. As the Germans understand, what they call 'Ostalgie' is not nostalgia for the Stasi but for decent pensions. Both get wrapped up in a Hobbesian left, an image of strong states and industrial battalions and the stability of secure wages and a social safety net. The Cold War reminds us of that world, even (perhaps especially) those of us from lands far from the direct experience of the brutality of any 'socialist' secret police.

This sympathetic romance of the past provides the glue uniting apparently disparate phenomena. It is the noble wish to step out of this present, not to be caught up in it and a participant in it any longer. The alienation is sometimes spatial as much as temporal;

the veneration attaches itself to projects still alive now but faraway, as in the rolling sagas of Latin America's 'Pink Tide'. In both cases, distant phenomena are invoked in the face of local absences, and to defy the forms of belonging, the identities and coalitions, and so the assumed enemies, which together define regnant values drenched in blood. But the nature of the escape can look quite different in different places.

In Britain, whose Communist Party was never a national electoral force but held serious industrial significance, 'tankieism' means memories of brilliant and effective organisers like Bert Ramelson and Derek Robinson: 'Red Robbo', who terrified the press. They were sufficiently marginal to feel countercultural now, but sufficiently powerful to be the punchline of nobody's joke, which after 1989 sometimes felt like the necessary condition of radicals in the imperial core. Their disdain for factory and student Trotskyists fits nicely now into a protest against the pathetic and the tiny, paper-selling and small protests that lose, as the image of the left. They evoke the world of Negri's 'mass worker'. Corbynism, where the left once again promised to matter, easily invited the veneration of this earlier tradition for some.

In the United States, a different dynamic reigns. There, the anti-Communism that propels Fox News doggerel about the 'Franklin School' to the top of the bestseller lists arises simultaneously with a racist moral panic about Critical Race Theory. With some obvious partial exceptions – like the Black Panther Party – campism appeals there as a surpassing, more than a recovery, of a national tradition. It is tied above all to the language of anti-imperialism. It marks the moment of taking seriously *most of the world*, in a nation whose ignorance about others is matched only by the ferocity with which it bombs them.

If in the United States a largely white left is quick to dismiss the same Stalin whose name meant inspiration to black militants in Alabama in the 1930s and Vietnamese liberation fighters in the

1960s, and if in Britain a largely middle-class left is inclined to sneer at the same Stalin who inspired miners in Chopwell to rename their streets after Marx and Lenin, then it only seems reasonable to ask: 'what have you got instead?' And when the answers are wanting, when some on the left bury their heads to the defeat of world revolution and call still for freedom everywhere tomorrow, while others react to that loss by accommodating themselves to imperialist power as servile ministers or crowing chroniclers, people look elsewhere. From Nicaraguan Sandinistas to Longbridge car manufacturers, very different communities summon a future past, a defeated set of hopes once cherished by decent people struggling to end their degradation.

For campism, a virtuous alienation from our time and place means experiencing an affinity instead with a better land of struggle. But it must also mark failure: an age of holding Lenin tight since we do not have new Lenins reinventing emancipation in new colours fitted to new conditions, just as he did in the formation of proletarian internationalism and the electrifying call for soviet power a century ago. Amid the absence or weakness of such emancipatory subjects now, the ability to imagine alternative worlds is simply not sustained by real movements presenting the serious possibility of revolutionary transformation in the global North. But those who call socialism impossible, who dismiss the abolition of capitalism as an utterly absent project in today's politics, cannot deny that armies of millions pledged themselves in name to that goal not so long ago, and those armies lasted for decades! The turn away from the here and now evidences a real abyss, of which campism is but the symptom. The sad reformulation of radical politics, as we will now see, comes in the campists' relationship to the world they choose to inhabit instead.

The impotent present

In truth, all this can be very presentist: the new campism is new for its sometime abandonment of the trajectory towards global victory and universal dignity that gave to 1930s Communists and 1960s anti-colonial revolutionaries some justification for accepting present difficulties. The new campism venerates a past *without its future past*. Consider, for example, how the campism that defends ostensible Leninists around the world joins with or competes with another tendency. An apparently more forlorn campist realism would defend Assad or Putin or whoever else proclaims opposition to Washington with a big bureaucracy behind them, regardless of their Communist or even left credentials. There is a left Fukuyamaism there, where the only thing possible in this present of capitalist realism is to herald the violent authoritarians who frighten, at least, the very most violent power in the world[†].

We might call this *imperialist realism*. Within it, campism is appended to a thinner and more defensive project than before – then championing the end of capitalism, now avoiding asphyxiation by hegemonic powers – and on this view the best we can do is to choose between rival imperialisms. There is a determined miserabilism here that will not give up on tragedy; when revolutions really do break out, as in Syria, the insistence that all politics is geopolitics and so no emancipatory struggle is conceivable now becomes circular and self-validating. The politics of a nobler freedom is an impossibly fringe project today, we are told, so we must choose between imperial camps. And then when this politics does emerge, it is ruled out as a fraud, since the camps must be all there is. Look at Syria today, and the resources for such a conclusion are clear.

The great Caribbean anthropologist David Scott has seen a shift of genre between the 1938 and 1963 editions of CLR James' *Black*

[†] I take this term from Slavoj Zizek, who uses it to name the Third Way. Since Blair's 'war on terror', Clinton's 'war on crime' and Schroder's Hartz IV war on the poor more than confirmed their sometime self-designation as forces beyond the left, I think Zizek's appellation is inappropriate: these were simply Fukuyamaists. The tendency named in this article is a better candidate for the descriptor. There is a continuity between the two worth stressing, though. When Gordon Brown entered the British Treasury with an immediate plan to hand great power to the unelected Governor of the Bank of England, he did so on the explicit basis that a Labour government could only invest in saving the welfare state if it had the confidence of 'the markets', avoiding a run on sterling. This was, briefly, a sort of Left Fukuyamaism: a claim about the narrow possibilities for effective political action at the End of History, and an attempt to chart that narrow course against leftwing idealists who still dreamed of a world without bankers. Campism says the same of idealists who dream of a world without censorship and prison camps.

Jacobins, from the romance of revolution to its tragedy. In James' account of the modern world's first successful slave revolt, the Haitian revolution at the turn of the nineteenth century, its leaders send liberated slaves back to work on plantations after the old slavers are exiled. Haitians remain, on the day after the revolution, conscripted to a global capitalist division of labour, without the power to remake the whole world and so to find alternative means of feeding themselves. After their nominal victory they are besieged, despised and punished by all the powers of the world – slave-holders or colonial beneficiaries of brutalisation, all of them. It is fitting to our purposes here that James, a Trinidadian Trotskyist whose hostility to social domination radicalised him against empire and against Stalin too, commented on the isolation and degeneration of the Russian revolution through an analogy with Haiti.

Scott's *Omens of Adversity* has recently extended the same tragic narrative arc to cover the United States' devastation of revolutionary Grenada in the 1980s. Making a new world in the twentieth century was, not only in Russia but across Africa and Asia and the Americas, a project undertaken against the deliberate suffocations of concentrated power, which succeeded in strangling the possibility of a happy freedom for the oppressed. In Grenada today, Scott notes, there is one public memorial to the dreams of the New Jewel movement and their violent crushing by Reagan's forces. It is a memorial built by the US, honouring the US dead. He writes of its imposing arches, and its engraved claim that Grenadians are 'grateful' to their invaders:

> It seems to me hard not to recognize in it the embodiment of a cynical act of imperial power, the sneering reward empire offers to mark the defeat of a people's defiance. If on the one side the monument confronts us with the projection of overwhelming domination, on the other side, it registers the limp prostration of a defeated people's spirit.

In today's imperialist realism, this tragedy is keenly felt. The 'postcolonial' names the epoch after the death of many hopes in the *anti*-colonial age. In fact, the shift was global, the defeat of the long 1968. Scott's reflections might just as easily be trained on the swapping of Communist for National Front votes in 2000s France, or the immiserated wreckage of 1990s Russia, as 1980s Grenada. Campism owes its revival now not just to the political and cultural ubiquity of nostalgia, but also to a very contemporary condition: the desolation of past hopes. Campism offers a means of facing the present, not only running away from it. It appeals as a form of reassuring denial – all is not lost, China remains a vanguard of anti-imperialism, and so on – but also a different and subtler and altogether more compelling kind of forgetting. It stares into overwhelming defeat, wrought by the power of the vile masters of the universe, and to avoid rehashing all the pain it skips to the end of the story told by James and Scott. There is nothing in the world but the enemy's fortresses or ours, it says, though revolutionaries everywhere once dreamed bolder dreams: of freedom. We must pick a fortress, say campists, or we will have to sacrifice our loyalty to Haitian slaves and Russian workers whose struggles have ended here. The gulf between revolutionary hopes and grisly outcomes is thus repressed by this move. In forgetting that gap, campism avoids facing the fact of failure and so abdicates the task of working out how to do things better. It proved an apparently impossible task in the twentieth century, and Fukuyamaism says it always is so. In practice, campists agree. The final years of Lenin's life, his 'last struggle' in Moshe Lewin's construal, involved his grappling with the tragic implications of the following predicament: could it be that the disciplined, militarised defence of the workers' state necessitated abandoning the very conditions of real, democratic workers' rule that gave it its legitimacy and its potentially socialist character? Saving the workers' state in 1918-21 might have meant destroying it. In a set of desperate proposals against calcifying bureaucratisation and national chauvinism in the Bolshevik state apparatus, Lenin sought frantically to recover the sovereignty of the millions without whom socialism would be an empty husk.

The campists forget this, or simply choose – like everyone else at the End of History – to give up for now on such awkward idealism. In China, exploited workers and billionaires both sit under the red flag, so *something* has survived. The woe of the campist position amounts to this: staying true to a battered original hope means acceding to any leader born in its firmament, even as the revolution rots under them. Those who strive to remain true in some sense to older and bolder aspirations can appear to postcolonial campism as naïve or even as racists, unaware or blasé about the full trauma of imperial counter-revolution. But the critique of this politics that interests us here is all about reckoning more fully with the scale of the 'liberal democratic' horror, seeing the devastation of emancipatory horizons as its bitter fruit. Campists reduce the complex conditions of defeat to strangulation from outside, which functions like Trotskyist stories of betrayal to keep the project clean and avoid messier questions. But this is not a moralistic criticism of campism, or a call for an easy return to the grander projects whose rubble campists clasp. New campisms are of interest precisely as symptoms of real capitalist and imperialist wreckage, as streams at the margins that tell us things about our cultural and intellectual condition more generally.

One last feeling bears noting in this connection, which again reflects and rebels against the affective economy of our times. Aligning yourself with dictators overseas marries desires for radicalism and a particular kind of *reasonableness*. It means horrifying the defenders of a capitalist order you loathe while still internalising all their dismissiveness about silly and naïve dreamers. It also means giving up far too much. It means making the socialist offer to the world a lot of prisons and spies and the caste power of a state elite. 'I'm no stargazing kid', says the Stalinist to the sneering liberal: 'While you write poetry about democracy, I have the guts to defend millions of deaths as necessary. How's that for hard-headed realism?' That is to perform the kind of world-weary maturity praised since 1989 as the only un-embarrassing orientation to politics, outdoing the Right for cynicism and so gleefully claiming that terrain they thought was theirs while still finding an outlet for those undead desires, scorned as infantile, to break all the rules.

We are all tankies

The last part of the story is really the most fundamental. The pull in twentieth-century socialism was towards defining its object as 'the economy' and its instrument as the national state. That entailed understanding capitalism as a system of private ownership and market exchange counterposed to state ownership and distribution, rather than seeing capital as a structure of domination to be opposed in the name of freedom and popular power. Contemporary Stalinism is an instance and a symptom of that, just as social democracy is: twin forms (as Hal Draper had it) of 'socialism from above.' Some postcolonial state-building might be clustered under this label too, though often more ambivalently and complicatedly; in the genealogy of contemporary imperialist realism this plays a crucial role, but Western attempts to bundle enthusiasm for the FLN in Algeria with illusions in Brezhnev as identical forms of 'substitutionism' – making state apparatuses the agents of our politics and distant developments the only cause of hope – often worked to reveal the crudeness (or much worse) of the critics. Some state projects really did harbour more hope than others.

The challenge is to move beyond finger-wagging condemnation to take seriously the bind that produced a hundred years ago – East and West, North and South – this common trajectory towards the embrace of national states as socialist instruments and national economies as their objects for delivering not freedom but some modicum of economic equality: planning and full employment beyond the miserable vicissitudes of crises-ridden domination by the impersonal power of the marketplace. The language of this politics was creativity and stability at once, that distinctly modern faith in the mutability of the world to human design wielded here to advocate the grey planning of everything. Foucault was surely wrong to claim there has never been a 'socialist governmentality'. It is hard now to think ourselves out of this intellectual condition. At its dawn, socialist governmentality was a reply to the coming of universal suffrage in some places, the decline of transnational insurrectionary energies, the ascent of a bureaucratic state arsenal for the management of employment and distribution within the shell of capitalist states, and the burning challenges of poverty to which that new techne seemed to present ready answers. The socialist challenge and possibility, then, was to free the machinery of state management over the economy from its fragmentary, half-hearted deployment by capitalists worried about the invasion of their hallowed hidden abode.

The curious dialectic here involved the deployment and the adaptation of aspirations around power so important to Marx; in seeking to take control over an alienated social metabolism, represented increasingly as a 'blind' subject lurching from boom to bust, the agent of that control moved from millions to a few administrators. The desire for autonomous power over ourselves to replace hierarchical power over us thus metamorphosed into its opposite, by dint of changing historical possibilities more than any conspiracy. Trotsky's *Revolution Betrayed* is dangerously titled; his disciples cast Stalin or a set of bureaucrats as personal betrayers of the revolution, scapegoated in order to leave the socialist project untarnished, but Trotsky himself treated war and scarcity as pressures transforming and crippling the possibilities of the nascent USSR. Many on the left resisted the pull towards a top-down statified socialism, from council communists, syndicalists, autonomists and Luxemburgists to the most radical of the Non-Aligned internationalists – but they tended to be much worse at explaining its appeal, and so explaining their usual marginality. In fact, though they called for workers' councils not distant officials in suits, much of socialism's most radical fringe (Trotsky certainly included) was conquered too by the language of 'the economy' as a coherent site for capitalism and the modernist insistence on constant agency as the proper alternative to capital's invisible hand. That economism gradually let dreams of freedom narrow and then slide, while the veneration of agency allowed autonomous power to become hierarchical power. The dissidents tended to imagine sharp ruptures between their democratic ambitions and anti-democratic 'counterrevolutions' in the name of revolution; the blurred lines are the repressed in this thinking.

Today, the newly expansive language of 'abolition' – against police, prisons, borders, the family, work and even the value-form – evokes the salutary rediscovery of a leftism defined by insubordination against oppressive iterations of power and status[‡]. At best, this is even the recovery of ambitions to chart a 'free individuality' after capital, concentrating on domination and hierarchy as its enemies and so strikingly more emancipatory than Hobbesian praise for dictators. How, then, can it coexist with a new campism in the same moment? Both index an absence of agents and strategies sufficient to the task of freedom: 'abolition' begins by naming its enemies, where once the language of 'transition' foregrounded its subjects and its roadmap. Against the same backdrop, an irony greets the resurgence of campism's 'barracks socialism.' Its protagonists are sometimes coolly aware of the irony, which is what makes them meaningfully novel, and explains their embrace of the kitsch aesthetic. The revival comes after the *desolation* of the twentieth century constellation that established the original campism as plausible. Its camp (be it the Warsaw Pact in the East, or the Non-Aligned Movement as a meaningfully radical actor in the South) is gone, and so is the Fordism that once made it a mass politics in the North and West.

Campism was founded in a claim about the deflection of class struggles into geopolitical struggles. Long before the tanks rolled into Hungary in 1956, 1939 was its watershed. That year, Communists grit their teeth and defended Stalin's desperate pact with the Nazi state that would put them in concentration

---

‡ It is worth remembering, though, as testament to the complexities of the twentieth century – where dreams of freedom became bound up with its opposite, because the road to socialism was so strewn with obstacles that illusions or clear-eyed bargains seemed to many necessary to avoid despair or fatalism – that Angela Davis could call for the abolition of prisons in the US and then praise the prison system in East Germany. And yet: as the Soviet Union dissolved, Davis was an anti-Stalinist dissident inside the Communist Party.

camps, since the endurance of socialism – of a world even vaguely liveable, amid the Depression and fascism – hinged, it seemed to them, on the defence of the Soviet Union. After the defeat of world Communism, in a 1994 interview, Eric Hobsbawm had the dubious privilege of attempting to explain this to Michael Ignatieff, whose haughty liberalism soon saw him calling for bombs over Baghdad. How, asked this bastion of peaceful moderation, could intelligent people have committed themselves to such violent idealism? It was, Hobsbawm corrected him, always a sombre kind of politics; survival was its language more than utopia. But it was possible too for twentieth-century Communists to believe that new and better worlds really were in the offing in the East. Trotsky insisted on the defence of Stalin's Soviet Union in any war with imperialist powers – magical thinking was not the only alternative to campism – but official Communists refused his pained choice with a clearer-cut one: in Stalingrad there was socialism, or at least there *might be soon*, and it was worth defending as such. Today, that illusion is easily enough dispelled, and not only by the implosion of the Soviet project. Domination by wage-labour, which provided the core of Marx's critique of capital, remained in force across the Warsaw Pact even at its height. The alienation of our powers to a distant state apparatus, planning an industrial society in the Fordist mould, is not the proper horizon of emancipatory politics. It was far from the goal of the most romantic Communists and anti-imperialists whose faces adorn the campist repertoire.

All of this is close to irrelevant, though, once campism is transformed by a turn from optimism to pessimism. Today, it is less often a naïve claim about distant realities than a cynical one about ours. Oppressive states are to be defended not only from British and American bombs but from domestic revolutions too, not because they are great but because nothing great is possible. This politics emerges from the same conditions that birth the vampire castle, whose quest for safe spaces in an unsafe world only marks a different response to despair. Campism's left critics, from blood-stained social democrats to purer revolutionaries, usually fail to own up to the impasse it addresses, which is the coexistence of savage imperial hegemony and a desperate need for some counterweight to it. The critique of this campism should involve a lot of sympathy, or it becomes suspect. At times, campism can demand the brutal denigration of radicals and revolutionaries in inconvenient places, from Prague to Aleppo. But at other moments, it becomes clear that campists want to love in a world that makes it hard to love; they want to cherish flawed projects and to herald the bravery of their protagonists, from Soviet futurisms amid a crumbling old world to the hopeful boldness of Cultural Revolution, and from Kwame Nkrumah and Thomas Sankara to the *campesinos* of Latin American revolution. In fact, campism is caught in a co-dependence of love and denigration, where the violence of our world seems to render love possible only through some nasty exclusions. What if it is true that North Korean technology delivered arms to Palestinian fighters – that without the Kim dictatorship they would be weaker in Gaza? What to do with this fact, once we accept (some campists still don't, and so repress the problem, but others do) that Kim starves and tortures as the palace-dwelling warden of an open-air prison? Contemporary campism inhabits the tension which, in very different ways, we must learn to inhabit too: between well-grounded gloom and much-needed faith.

The campists are right, not about the states they defend or the revolutions they condemn or defile, but about this. They bear witness to the awkwardness that accompanies talk of hope and freedom and equality today. In a sense, they embrace the recognition that these are strange and foreign terms now, and so in wielding them they choose to sound like cynics and not like the feebler ingenue. Here we might return with sympathy even to the worst of the online provocateurs, with their drawling over Beria, designed to shock. They announce their yearning for another world, and in the same breath they almost wink, 'I'm joking!' In the end, this is a lot of bravado to evade a choice we all shirk in our different ways. Perhaps they think the barrel bombs and re-education camps of a global 'war on terror' mark an almost incomprehensible tragedy, in which criminal states like Syria and China must be defended with eyes wide open, because nothing better than butchery is possible.

In this case, they are conservatives mourning the End of History, since Fukuyamaism is liberal or conservative. But there cannot really be a Fukuyamaism that is actively *left-wing*. This might be the melancholia which jibes and jokes about Stalin's machismo are supposed to cover. Or perhaps the truth is something else. Perhaps, like the rest of us, they want ways to give doubt a rest.

PATTY PAINE

Selected Images

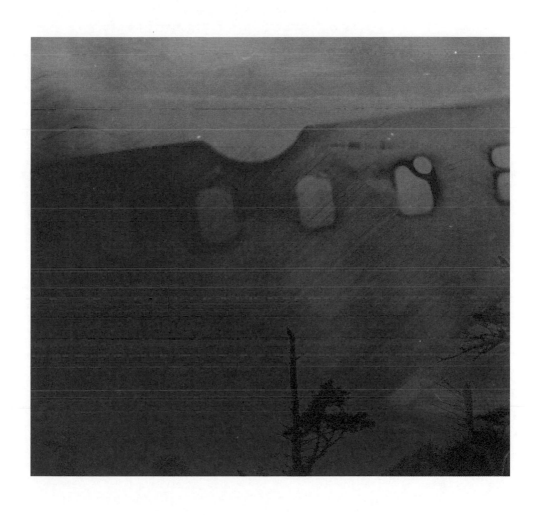

TITLES

Vacant 35MM NEGATIVE, DEVELOPED THEN CHEMICALLY ALTERED.

Widow POLAROID PHOTO, ALTERED THROUGH EMULSION MANIPULATION.

Door Two POLAROID PHOTO, ALTERED THROUGH EMULSION MANIPULATION.

Penitent 35MM NEGATIVE, DEVELOPED THEN CHEMICALLY ALTERED.

Post Empire 35MM NEGATIVE, DEVELOPED THEN CHEMICALLY ALTERED.

Nationless POLAROID PHOTO, ALTERED THROUGH EMULSION MANIPULATION.

Against Memory POLAROID PHOTO, ALTERED THROUGH EMULSION MANIPULATION.

Harvest POLAROID PHOTO, ALTERED THROUGH EMULSION MANIPULATION.

Mute 35MM NEGATIVE, DEVELOPED THEN CHEMICALLY ALTERED THEN HANDPAINTED.

Elegy 35MM NEGATIVE, DEVELOPED THEN CHEMICALLY ALTERED.

This is How We Vanish 35MM NEGATIVE, DEVELOPED THEN CHEMICALLY ALTERED.

Torn 35MM NEGATIVE, DEVELOPED THEN CHEMICALLY ALTERED.

SARAH JAFFE

Nothing and Everything: Mourning Against Work

When my father died it changed everything.

I crashed head-first into grief about a year and a half before everyone else I know joined me in it. It turned my life upside down, wrung me out, and left me alone with nothing left to give even though I kept trying. I kept thinking that grief was something I could solve, could ace like a test or a work assignment, that preparation and strength and labour could bring me out. It did not work that way.

I hoped that I could write my way through it, that words on paper or a computer screen would provide the salve that they always had. I filled notebooks, scraps of napkin stuffed in my bag, began and abandoned documents, wrote email drafts to myself that linger like ghosts when I open a drafts folder and see fragments of who I was then. I could write, yes, but I could not make it make sense, and I could not make it stop.

Grief is not a thing we do; it is a thing that happens to us. It is a thing that overwhelms us, that demands to be sat with, and lived through, and experienced, and felt, and that goes against everything the world we live in tells us. We are taught to work through things. We think there is a linear path. We assume we can do something to grieve, but the uncomfortable reality is that grief is a call to do nothing. And doing nothing makes us – well, most of us, who are expected to be productive labourers – extraneous. It makes us a problem.

It is near-universally agreed that there are 'stages' to grief, but one friend-in-loss stopped me short with the observation, 'What they don't tell you about the stages is that sometimes they hit you all at once.' Grief is not a staircase you climb or an elevator that ascends floor by floor. The assumption that this process, or indeed anything about being a human, can possibly unfold sequentially is, when you scratch it, so much more ideology. Grief will teach you that it simply does not work that way.

grief is nothing and everything all at once, inexpressible, and when you do try to express it it comes out in so many clichés, it dwells in the chest and flavours your breath and burrows into the pathways of your brain: nothing will be good again the worst has happened and therefore will keep happening. you have no control. you move through fog, one delicate step after another, unable to see where you are going, going anywhere at all seems ridiculous.

Grief is and is not a political issue in this way; it is complicated by being so personal, so physical, so embodied, so animal. And yet. It stalks all of our political arguments, haunts our praxis. 'Heartbreak is at the heart of all revolutionary consciousness,' Gargi Bhattacharyya writes. We turn to the struggle because we cannot do otherwise, so often, because we have been broken or watched others break on the cruel torture-wheel of capitalist society. And we find ourselves stuck, melancholic, lost when the struggle fails to materialise the way we dreamt it might. We tell ourselves, in the words of Joe Hill, 'Don't mourn, organise', but that is a command made of bravado, given by the martyr.

Freud asks 'What is the work that mourning performs?'

I read Freud in a pandemic lockdown winter in a borrowed New York City apartment that was always cold, the wind whipping off the East River forming a wind tunnel among the new buildings when I went outside masked and bundled against the weather and the virus. Sitting down with *Mourning and Melancholia* wrapped in a blanket, struggling through lockdown-induced brain fog, trying as always to turn my emotions into thoughts as though that would allow me more control. I wanted more than anything an answer to Freud's question, because if there was an answer to it, if I could identify that work, then I could do more of it faster and be healed.

But I was disappointed. Freud argues of the process of mourning that 'reality-testing has revealed that the beloved object no longer exists, and demands that the libido as a whole sever its bonds with that object', that in this process 'each individual memory and expectation in which the libido was connected to the object is adjusted and hyper-invested, leading to its detachment from the libido'. Mourning, in other words, is about letting go of the past, about detaching desire from memory. There is in this definition the 'expectation' as well as memory, but this feels underdeveloped, incomplete.

Or rather, it seemed a bad description of what was happening, by then, to the world, to everyone except those in the deepest denial (which is, supposedly, one of those 'stages of grief'). We were stuck inside, alone – even the tepid rituals of mourning still common in 2020s Western countries denied us. We could not see the death unless it happened to someone immediately touching us. The closest I got was talking over and over to nurses and healthcare workers, who told me of the layers of protective equipment they were piling on day after day, the grimness of holding a tablet so that family could say goodbye via FaceTime. We knew the deaths were happening, we were grieving human touch and all the other semblances of normal life that kept us feeling anything like ok, and yet we were supposed to just go on. Keep working. It was the stuckness that I kept returning to.

I had expected, before my father died, before I read Freud, that grief would be about the past. That processing the loss would be reeling through memories and crying a lot and generally being very sad. Freud describes it thus:

> Serious mourning, the reaction to the loss of a loved one, contains the same painful mood, the loss of interest in the outside world – except as it recalls the deceased – the loss of ability to choose any new love-object – which would mean replacing the mourned one – turning away from any task that is not related to the memory of the deceased.

Which is both accurate and painfully inadequate. I was not dwelling in memories as much as I was unable to imagine anything at all. What grief seemed to be more than anything was the loss of my future. A sufficiently close loss seemed to have taken all forward motion with it. Sometimes life seemed almost normal, and then it would require me to make a decision and I would be frozen. Stuck.

What if, then, grief is actually about the future? What if 'the work of mourning' is in fact letting go, not of the attachment, but of the future that you thought you would have, and what if the most painful, the least possible part is that you have to learn, while in the midst of hell, how to imagine a different future and to make it?

sometimes grief manifests as a simmering rage all through your body, the slightest thing liable to send you snapping into a tearful screaming reply: what the fuck do you want, who do you think you are, can't you see? but they cannot see, there is no recognised period of mourning, no widow's weeds to wear, no warning label, just the surfeit of emotion bubbling through you there is just the uncontrollable anger.

I think I prefer Mother Jones' admonition to 'Pray for the dead and fight like hell for the living' to Joe Hill's dictum. Jones, after all, even at her age, had no inclination toward martyrdom (if she did understand self-promotion long before the age of the personal brand). I am not one for prayer, but there is at least some acknowledgement in it that we do after all owe something to the dead, and, through them, to ourselves.

As I was working on this piece I got the news that Dawn Foster had died. It is one of the many bad clichés of grief-talk that it hits like a punch in the gut so shall we say rather that it made me want to punch others instead? Dawn's friends mourned on social media, and some of her enemies chose to celebrate. While it is, as many said, a sign of a life well-lived and the right fights picked that she had angered such ghouls, it is still disgusting.

We abide by too many sickly-sweet rules around death because we lack the real communal practices to honour it properly. And yet the picture of the comfortable celebrating the loss of a young working-class woman who had had the temerity to challenge their power was so repugnant because even in her death they sought to diminish her, to put her in her place and through her everyone who mourned her.

It is the hollowed-out starkness of moments like these that spark revolutions. We live through so many little losses, small wounds every day and keep going, have little choice in the matter anyway. But some losses are too big, and too cruel, and yet too emblematic of the way the world works. The callousness of the officer who killed George Floyd and the others who watched – the bravery of the teenage girl who filmed it all – touched off a rebellion that echoed across oceans. We do not know, always, which moments will be the ones that light the fuse; all we know is that our grief threatens to consume us. But, perhaps, we can turn it outward.

'Who can imagine another world unless they already have been broken apart by the world we are in?' Bhattacharyya asked.

Yes, grief flattens, it erases, it traps. But it also, in moments, opens up a vast space of new possibility. With so much less to lose, could we imagine something totally different? Could we imagine life absolutely otherwise? Could we all, if we seized time for our grief rather than shambling on like zombies, imagine collectively something new?

if you think of grief as a strike perhaps it will make sense, it seems at times that your body is on strike, you experience it as a loss of breath; then you realise that you are holding your breath yourself, you learn eventually to exhale deeply when you feel that tightening in your chest to tell your body to relax it isn't under fire or rather under water you don't need to preserve oxygen for the next onslaught. Somatically, the body remembers what it did to survive trauma and it tries to recreate that survival.

Freud notes, 'It is also most remarkable that it never occurs to us to consider mourning as a pathological condition and present it to the doctor for treatment, despite the fact that it produces severe deviations from normal behaviour.'

That might have been true when he wrote it, not too far removed from the ostentatious mourning periods of European dynasties and the new bourgeoisie. But these days, as Will Davies writes in *The Happiness Industry*, grief is just one more problem to be medicated away.

> One of the last remaining checks on the neurochemical understanding of depression was the exemption attached to people who were grieving: this, at the very least, was still considered a not unhealthy reason to be unhappy.

That was all wiped out with the advent of Wellbutrin – approved for use in the US in 1985 – which promised to alleviate 'major depressive symptoms occurring shortly after the loss of a loved one.' Grief is now a diagnosable mental illness if it lasts more than an acceptable period of time. Never mind your mourning, pop a pill and get back to work.

And then there is the question of the appropriate object of grieving. We are allowed, for a suitable time period, of course, to mourn relationships that make sense to the rules of capitalism: the nuclear family, pretty much. We are allowed to mourn the end of a marriage, the death of a parent, perhaps especially the death of a child. Grandparents, sure, though too much feeling will be seen as excessive. If a friend dies we get maybe a few weeks of support and then are expected to move on. And to mourn the breakup of a friendship, a not-really-family family member, a person whose relationship to you does not fit into these neat little boundaries, is seen as excessive, a waste of energy. Why do you care so much? It's not like it was your boyfriend, your wife. To mourn the loss of a stranger is flat-out unreasonable, even when those losses pile up, 100,000, 600,000 Covid-19 deaths, the uncountable death toll of the 'war on terror', 36 million deaths to AIDS. To sit with the vastness of these horrors and to let yourself even try to feel them is a disruption to our ideals of productivity. It is un-possible, perhaps inevitably in our psyche, but even more so to a system that requires us to keep working even as things fall apart around us, even as we fall apart, ourselves.

The lack of time and consideration for grief in particular is built into the capitalist mode of production, which cannot care if humans die. Capitalism cannot pause for death or accommodate the inherent weakness, frailty, and emotionality of human bodies. The dead can no longer produce value for capital; the living have too many inconvenient feelings about death. This is why Marx returned so often to metaphors of vampires, of undeath, and why robot panic hits us cyclically and existentially. We understand somewhere deep in our bones that this system would prefer robots to us, that labour-discipline would make robots of us.

The workers at Frito-Lay's factory in Topeka, Kansas walked out on strike this summer after over a year of 'essential' pandemic labour making snack foods, forced overtime shifts they call 'suicide' shifts. One worker wrote of seeing a colleague die right on the line. 'You had us move the body and put in another co-worker to keep the line going.' Another worker's father died of Covid-19 and she couldn't hold a service because of lockdown restrictions. 'You told her since there wasn't a funeral she didn't qualify for bereavement time. She had to take off two of her own days to grieve.'

This is telling, of course: we were denied funerals by pandemic conditions themselves created by the extension of capital to all corners and all habitats of the world, and without the brief socially-sanctioned ritual, we were expected simply not to grieve at all. The expectation once again that grief is just another form of work we do, and, without the performance, we must continue, unaffected.

The pandemic provided new opportunities for capital accumulation, particularly in the tech sector. Zoom's stock reached the stratosphere, aided by Amazon Web Services, as web video suddenly mediated all of our I-love-yous and goodbyes, as well as our endless hellish work meetings where we were expected to pretend nothing was wrong. Zoom funerals – I attended two – and mourning rituals simply did not substitute for the real thing. Facebook and the like had already sought to commodify human contact, to rank and categorise all of our relationships, but now we were truly stuck, depending on the attenuated possibilities offered to us by tech-mediated contact. Our relationships with one another interrupted by the screen.

Marx famously wrote, 'Capital is dead labour, which, vampire-like, lives only by sucking living labour, and lives the more, the more labour it sucks.' Capital is always pushing us beyond the merely human, even as it needs our living bodies. Even as late capitalism invaded our minds and hearts and turned our feelings into one more source of profit, it sought too to standardise those feelings, freeze our smiles into something inhuman because unchanging.

Capitalism cannot allow for feelings that cannot be boxed. It cannot admit to human finitude any more than it can admit that there are limits beyond which it cannot push this planet. It cannot let us grieve.

This is why grieving collectively becomes revolutionary. What is a radical politics without consideration of these universal pains and struggles? What is it without making space for joy, yes, but also pain? What is it if not a demand that we stop that murderous process in order to acknowledge the toll it has taken?

Even if we could not see the death toll Covid-19 wrought in order to grieve, everywhere it has left us reminders that we are only essential as so much blood and muscle and nerve to be exploited. Over and over politicians told us to keep going. Texas Lieutenant Governor Dan Patrick said that grandparents would cheerily die to keep the economy going: 'There are more important things than living.' Boris Johnson apparently opposed an autumn lockdown because 'the people dying are essentially all over 80'. Lives that were not productive were also not grievable; the old and the incarcerated, the ill and the disabled. 'Morbid' isn't a strong enough word for the voracious way the commentariat and Twitter trolls alike sought evidence that the dead deserved their fate because of some pre-existing conditions. We became little nations of insurance adjustors, seeking reasons to stamp onto the dead: compassion denied. Value denied.

the thing about absolutely gutwrenching rock-bottom grief is that getting out of it briefly makes just living on an even keel feel blissful and something to be savoured, your body feels alive again, sore feet, muscles straining, a slight sore throat and the desire unsatisfied at the pit of your belly feel amazing, the knowledge that it could flatten you again at any time that makes you hungry for this brief flare of life, save it, save it, capture it now while you can.

The world is on fire as I write this and yet as so many have noted, mostly the wrong things are burning. Yet some fires express grief, like the Catholic churches set on fire in Canada after the discovery of the unmarked graves of more than 1,000 First Nations children at former Church and state-backed 'residential schools', where Indigenous children were taken to have their culture beaten out of them. (Noted radical publication the *Economist* began its story on the discovery of the graves, 'The purpose of Canada's residential schools for indigenous children was to "kill the Indian in the child". Sometimes the child died too.') In the wake of the revelations, nearly two dozen churches were vandalised or burned, many of them on First Nations land. Prime Minister Justin Trudeau's response, that 'burning down churches is actually depriving people who are in need of grieving and healing and mourning from places where they can grieve and reflect and look for support' was the perfect finger-wagging reminder that grief is only acceptable if it is orderly and mannered and within approved walls, when the truth is of course that grief is anything but contained. Anything but containable.

These deliberate fires sit uneasily alongside the fires sparked by the record-shattering heat wave in June and July and then August, when the town of Lytton, British Columbia, first marked Canada's highest-ever temperature of 49.6°C and then was consumed by flames, trees and homes alike baked into so much kindling. In one video posted by residents fleeing the blaze, black smoke and orange flame curl and spiral menacingly toward the road, debris flying, the air a haunting grey-green, the title of the clip – 'Fleeing 'Q'emcin aka Lytton' – reminds us that this town too was built on the bones of the colonised, if not quite so literally.

Harsha Walia, organiser and author and fierce opponent of all this violence, stepped down from her job after using a common Internet-ism, 'burn it all down', in response to the latest horrors, an Internet-ism that captures the very real rage of a generation with no future and very little present beyond the virtual.

The fires remind me how useless all of that is.

you cry, or more often you cannot cry but sit in silent rage, the emotions stuck in a place in your chest near but not quite in your heart the feelings echo around your hollow insides, pounding away as they seek escape, but when they reach the place where they might find a way out instead they hover. The tears don't come. There are no words. You simply wait.

When I began to write this it was 'Freedom Day' in England, when the government decided to lift all Covid-19 protective measures and throw the doors open wide even as Covid-19 cases spiked around the world (including in England) and Richard Branson went up in a rocket and then Jeff Bezos did too and new oil fields were opening up despite the fires.

Climate activists in Scotland occupied a government building demanding a halt to the approval of drilling off the Shetland Islands. They would not stop the fires or the floods that came later in the summer, to cities I once called home. Nothing I could do and nothing they could do would change the immediate weather. And yet. It is with those people who act beyond the grief, despite the grief, no, more accurately, within the grief that I can find something other than despair. My grief was made manageable by people who loved me and people who barely knew me, who reached out with words and jokes and poetry and fierce hugs and voice notes and wordless care that reminded me that I was human, alive, not alone. And most importantly, that it was alright to feel emptied of all volition. To take time in the quiet to find myself before I could move was also a little revolution. Grief requires that we stand in the ashes and the rubble, accept it with our whole hearts, and then slowly take step after step forward anyway.

KEVIN OCHIENG OKOTH

The Darker Shades of Green

Post-war Germany has had its share of political scandals, from corruption and financial misconduct to treason and assassination. In comparison, the 'scandal' that derailed the Greens' campaign for the 2021 *Bundestagswahl* (federal election) was relatively minor: the party's candidate, Annalena Baerbock, stood accused of plagiarising large sections of her most recent book. The book – titled *Jetzt* (Now) to point to the immediacy of the challenges the country faces and the response required – was intended as an unofficial manifesto, outlining the policies her party would implement if given the mandate to form a government. Instead, controversy around the book foreshadowed electoral struggles to come. While the German public is usually quick to forget about financial, political or other kinds of transgression, the accusations against Baerbock stuck. (The sexist media discourse about her 'inexperience' and 'incompetence' certainly didn't help.)

Even as she performed well in interviews and debates leading up to the September election, it became increasingly clear that the next chancellor of the Federal Republic would not, as many had thought only a few months before, be a Green.

In mid-June Baerbock and Greens co-leader Robert Habeck unveiled the party's proposal for a 'social, ecological reconstruction' with a manifesto focused on the pressing issue of climate change. In her book, Baerbock had argued that Germany needed a fresh start after sixteen years of Merkel; and on the topic of climate change, Baerbock and her colleagues were ready to depart from grand coalition (CDU/CSU and SPD) orthodoxy with a call for an ecological transformation modelled on the Green New Deal. Curiously, the only coalition capable of turning the Greens' ambitious climate programme into actual policy – a red-red-green coalition of the Greens, SPD and Die Linke – was ruled out before the election: in an interview with the *Süddeutsche Zeitung*, Baerbock insisted that the Greens could not coalition with a party that threatened 'transatlantic relations' i.e., Germany's NATO membership. Former Greens chairman Cem Özdemir went even further, accusing Die Linke of having an inconsistent approach to human rights; unlike Die Linke, he argued, the Greens would never support dictators. (He was referring, of course, to Die Linke's foreign policy approach to Putin's Russia.) Under pressure from the Greens, Die Linke backtracked and removed the requirement for a German NATO exit from its programme. But the damage had already been done. And the question of how a coalition that didn't include the left would be capable of pressuring German industrialists into adopting a Green New Deal remained unanswered.

The Christian Democrats (CDU) and their Bavarian sister party the Christian Social Union (CSU) had predictably little to say about climate change. Armin Laschet, the lethargic and uncharismatic conservative candidate for chancellor, stubbornly refused to acknowledge that disasters like the recent floods, which killed over 180 people in North Rhine-Westphalia (NRW), are likely to become more frequent. (In 2021, flooding has already cost the German state over €30 billion.) Laschet's handling of the flooding crisis as *Ministerpräsident* (prime minister) of NRW was symptomatic of how little the conservatives cared: Laschet was spotted in the background of a television broadcast laughing and joking while *Bundespräsident* (president) Frank-Walter Steinmeier solemnly addressed the victims of the floods and their families. But this wasn't the first time Laschet had been under fire for his handling of climate politics. In 2018, Laschet and the state government of NRW deployed armed police to the Hambacher Forst, removing activists who were obstructing the opening of a new coal mine that was planned in the Rhineland forest, to appease the German multinational energy company RWE. To get permission to clear the site, the state government argued that the tree houses activists had built were a fire hazard and had to be removed to prevent forest fires. But a Cologne court later ruled that the eviction was illegal. To make matters worse, the Laschet-approved forest raid led to the death of journalist and filmmaker Steffen Meyn, who fell to his death from a tree house. Once again it was clear where the CDU/CSU stood on the climate crisis: with German capital and against leftist eco activists.

In the run up to the elections, the CDU/CSU wasn't looking much like the party that Germans had come to know during the Merkel years. Factional infighting – Bavarian prime minister, Markus Söder, was convinced that Laschet was too unpopular to win the election, and many in the CSU felt that it was the party's turn to field a candidate – ensured that there was little support for Laschet among his colleagues in the South-East. Yet even within his own party, Laschet was beginning to lose support due, in part, to his deteriorating public image. The same week a twenty-year-old petrol station clerk was shot dead by a customer (who was so angered by the clerk's request to wear a mask that he went all the way back home to pick up his gun and return to the petrol station) Laschet's team uploaded a campaign video showing him having a cordial conversation with a member of the Querdenker, the movement of 'corona sceptic' hippies, anti-vaxxers, far-right conspiracy theorists, AfD supporters and libertarian ideologues that has taken Germany by storm. When confronted about the video, Laschet brushed aside any criticism, arguing that the CDU was willing to reason with everyone, even those with a 'critical attitude' towards the country's handling of the pandemic. Seemingly unbothered by the murder in Idar-Oberstein, Laschet continued to cosy up to the far-right in the hopes that the CDU/CSU could benefit from the AfD's (Alternative for Germany) stagnation. But could the marriage of convenience between what Alberto Toscano has described as anti-democratic 'fascisms of freedom' with the ordoliberal politics of the conservatives really enable the CDU/CSU to lure voters away from the far-right?

In late July, Oliver Nachtwey joked that the federal election would be decided by which party ran the more disastrous campaign. And as the Greens and the CDU/CSU duked it out over whose campaign would take the title, the SPD stood back and watched. By doing absolutely nothing, the party regained its momentum and surged in the polls. Earlier in the year, when the SPD was polling at a dismal 15 per cent, the conversation around who would succeed Merkel focused on two names: Armin Laschet and Annalena Baerbock. By late August, however, the SPD had gained 10 per cent in the polls and 53 per cent of Germans said they could imagine Olaf Scholz as their next chancellor. Considering the very un-Social Democratic behaviour Scholz had become known for – supporting the Hartz IV labour market reforms under the SPD government of Gerhard Schröder, his role in the Cum-Ex tax avoidance scandal as mayor of Hamburg, or his failure in handling the Wirecard fiasco (arguably the most high-profile financial scandal in the country's post-war history) – this was somewhat surprising. But for many, Scholz was the man who had saved millions of jobs by placing workers on short-time work allowance programmes during the financial crisis of 2008 and approved a stimulus package of over €1 trillion during the coronavirus crisis. In other words, Scholz was a reliable Social Democrat, an image that was reinforced by his reserved civil servant demeanour. (The *Süddeutsche Zeitung* described Scholz as a 'man who leaves nothing up to chance and would rather say nothing than say something wrong'.) And by mid-September, it looked likely that this was enough to convince German voters that he was the right man for the job.

Linksruck Verhindern

As the final results came in there were few surprises: the SPD narrowly claimed victory, coming in at 25.7 per cent, only 1.6 per cent above the CDU and around 10 per cent ahead of the Greens, who slipped just below 15 per cent. Of course, the CDU's strategy of outflanking the AfD on the right failed miserably. The example of Hans-Georg Maaßen, the ultra-conservative former president of the *Verfassungsschutz* (Federal Office for the Protection of the Constitution) was symptomatic: Maaßen only finished second in his constituency, losing out to SPD candidate Frank Ullrich and coming in only a few percentage points before the AfD. Maaßen, an AfD-clone who counted far-right extremists and Neo Nazis among his closest supporters, ran in the Thuringia constituency of Suhl-Schmalkalden-Meiningen-Hildburghausen-Sonneberg to show that the CDU shared the concerns of the *besorgte Bürger* (concerned citizens, as far-right conspiracy theorists like to refer to themselves). The fact that Maaßen has previously been under fire for denying that the death of a German man in Chemnitz had led to increased violence against 'foreigners' in the city, made him seem like the perfect candidate; but instead it was the SPD who emerged victorious in the CDU (and AfD) bastion. In fact, the SPD was the strongest party in three of the five *Neue Bundesländer* (the federal states that became part of the BRD after reunification) – a surprising result considering the party's sobering performance in the East in 2017. But in 2021, Brandenburg, Mecklenburg-Western Pomerania and Saxony-Anhalt looked surprisingly red.

For the moment, the forward march of the AfD in the East has been halted. But the other two states are still dominated by the AfD: in Saxony and Thuringia, the party captured 24.6 per cent and 24 per cent of the votes, respectively. Still, the SPD came in at a close second with 19.3 per cent and 23.4 per cent, respectively, which was an astonishing improvement on 8.7 and 10.2 per cent in 2017, and compared well to the AfD's sober 'gains' of -2.4 and 11.3 per cent. The AfD's (relative) weakness can partly be attributed to infighting between a far-right faction led by Alice Weidel and Tino Chrupella, and a national conservative wing led by Jörg Meuthen who bitterly disagreed on whether members with close ties to neo Nazis should be excluded. (The case of Matthias Heinrich – an AfD politician who shared photos of himself with description: 'the friendly face of the NS [national socialism]' – is yet to be resolved.) But there have also been some discrepancies between the AfD's public profile and its candidates' personal lives. As Richard Seymour points out, 'the new far right is particularly galvanised by a conspiracy theory which believes [...] "gender ideology" is destroying civilisation'. For proponents of such theories, he argues, deviant sexual relationships threaten the reproduction of European societies through the traditional family; thus LGBT people are to blame for Europe's low birth rates and the process of 'white extinction'. But, despite the AfD's vow to protect the traditional European family of mother, father and children from the threat of 'gender ideology', its top candidate, Alice Weidel, lives openly with her partner – a Swiss woman of Sri-Lankan descent – in a gay relationship.

Yet this hasn't prevented the AfD from increasing its share of the youth vote in the East. In Saxony-Anhalt, for example, the party only finished in third place, behind both SPD and CDU; but it still managed to gain votes among eighteen- to twenty-nine-year-olds. *Die Zeit* argued that the AfD's large share of the youth vote could be explained by the party's ability to speak to the social and economic anxieties that have only gotten worse during the coronavirus crisis. (Almost three quarters of AfD voters in Saxony-Anhalt see themselves as economically stable but downwardly mobile, and believe they are witnessing a deterioration of living standards both in their area and in Germany more broadly. According to a study by the Institut für Demoskopie in Allensbach, 42 per cent of young people polled in the East felt this way compared to a much lower 19 per cent in the West.) But the AfD cannot be easily dismissed as a protest party. In local campaigns in rural areas, the party toned down some of its neoliberal and anti-immigration rhetoric to focus on issues such as preserving sports clubs or local libraries and making public transport more affordable. To young people outside of cities these aren't fringe concerns: as Kerstin Völkl of the University of Halle in Saxony argues, 'right-wing parties know how to capitalise on the fact that the bus only comes once or twice a day and that the internet doesn't work'. Such social alienation thus allows far-right organisations to mobilise young people through sports and youth clubs, and to show that they take their concerns seriously.

Surprisingly, the Free Democrats (FDP) were the most popular party among first-time voters nationally, ahead of even the Greens and the AfD. This was unexpected for a party that notoriously doesn't give a shit about young people: as a party of high earners and the professional classes, there aren't many young Germans who stand to benefit from the FDP's dogmatic neoliberalism. But through its effective use of social media – there is a whole genre of pro-FDP memes on Instagram – and by positioning itself as a party of the future, the FDP won over young voters in the West. Young Germans, it seems, were all too aware of the limits of Merkel's moderate politics and believed that another grand coalition government would be ill-equipped to deal with the economic and social challenges the country faces. Moreover, a *Financial Times* profile of young voters from early September showed that the lockdown and Merkel's handling of the coronavirus crisis was an important factor: many felt let down by her lacklustre response to their – quite serious – concerns. The fact that the FDP was the only party apart from the AfD and the Querdenken-affiliated Die Basis to directly oppose the coronavirus lockdowns – and the only one that did without drifting into the realm of conspiracy theory – further shows how well the anti-Merkel strategy worked to mobilise the youth. For a generation of *Merkelkinder* (young people who have not experienced any government other than Merkel's grand coalition in their lifetime) a vote for the FDP was a rejection of continuity.

The FDP's electoral success also meant that Christian Lindner, the free-market tech enthusiast who famously torpedoed coalition talks with the Greens and the CDU/CSU in 2017, emerged as a crucial power broker and front runner for the office of finance minister. As inequality continues to rise – both between East and West and low and high incomes – Lindner has called for the abolition of the *Solidaritätszuschlag* (a tax levied to finance the economic reconstruction of the East) claiming that it breaches the constitution. But abolishing the *Soli* would not provide any significant tax relief for the lowest 90 per cent of the population; only the top 10 per cent would truly benefit. As Lukas Scholle and Ines Schwerdtner explain in *Jacobin*, the *Soli* has effectively been (part) abolished for incomes up to €74,000 and only applies in full for incomes upwards of €110,000. But this isn't the most worrying aspect of Lidner's politics; far more concerning is his support for the *Schuldenbremse* (debt brake) – an instrument of ordoliberal economic control written into the German constitution, which limits deficit spending to 0.35 per cent of GDP. Federal states were exempted from the *Schuldenbremse* during the coronavirus crisis, which allowed for much-needed public spending. But Lidner wants to bring the *Schuldenbremse* back into effect as quickly as possible while simultaneously cutting tax rates for high earners. In absence of steady economic growth, this would mean that federal states have less tax income to invest in basic services while having to impose austerity to meet the requirements of balanced budgets. This isn't very reassuring for cash-strapped communities struggling with crumbling social infrastructure.

In early September, Wolfgang Streeck described the 2021 election as 'more uncertain than ever in the history of the Federal Republic'. One thing, however, is certain: the coalition that will govern a post-pandemic Germany will not include the left. Or, as Loren Balhorn succinctly put it, 'the centre will hold'. The motto of all three contenders – Greens, SPD and CDU/CSU – seemed to be *linksruck verhindern* (the conservative and far-right slogan calling on voters to prevent a leftward shift). Thirty-one years after the collapse of the German Democratic Republic (GDR) and the fall of the Berlin Wall, the spectre of communism still haunts the Federal Republic (BRD) – or at least those who intend to further the project of Merkelism, that 'disastrously successful ruling class project' to borrow a phrase from Seymour, which has been a masterclass in the subtle brutalities of 'ordoliberal praxis'. In the right's red-baiting narrative – mainly propagated by the CDU/CSU and AfD, but bolstered by the Greens' demand that any viable coalition partner must express unequivocal support for NATO – communism still served as, in Seymour's words again, 'the name of the abyss, the pulpy mass of shit' which 'destroys hierarchies that are precious to social being, under the cover of democracy republicanism or "gender ideology"'. In other words, communism had to be prevented by any means necessary if continuity with Merkelism was to be achieved. But in what sense a red-red-green coalition could really be described as a gateway to communism – apart from Die Linke's roots in the ruling party of the GDR, a formation that could more accurately be described, following Steffen Mau, as a 'proletarian petit bourgeois society' – was never truly addressed. But this didn't stop the right from crying (communist) wolf.

But it didn't really take a coordinated right-wing effort to make the only party left of the SPD irrelevant; Die Linke managed that all by themselves. On 27 February, the party elected a new leadership at its party conference, ending the nine-year tenure of Katja Kipping and Bernd Rlexinger as party leaders. Their tenure had, of course, been marked by intense battles with a 'left-conservative' faction led by Sahra Wagenknecht (see 'Aufstehen's Populist Revolt' in *Salvage #8*). Could the new leadership of Janine Wissler, whom Loren Balhorn has described as a 'rising star on the party's left wing' and Susanne Hennig-Wellsow reinvigorate the party and finally move it beyond the 9 per cent it had stabilised, or rather stagnated, at in the last decade? Unfortunately, the change in leadership hasn't paid off: on a national level the party's share of votes declined by 4.3 per cent to a dismal 4.9 per cent. In fact, the party didn't even pass the 5 per cent hurdle (the electoral mechanism which prevents parties who gain fewer than 5 per cent of the vote from participating in the national government). But a technicality – three members of Die Linke won a direct mandate in their respective constituencies enabling the party to be represented in the *Bundestag*: Gregor Gysi, Gesine Lötzsch and Sören Pellman all managed to win their constituencies in the East – ensured that the party could be part of the opposition. In any case, Die Linke was no longer a viable coalition partner: due to the party's poor performance, Greens, SPD and Die Linke only combined for 363 of the 368 seats required to form a governing coalition.

In Berlin, where a red-red-green coalition has governed at state level since 2016, there was another major vote on Election Day, as Berliners voted in a referendum on whether Deutsche Wohnen & Co, Vonovia and Akelius & Co, the city's biggest landlords, should be expropriated. The Greens' Berlin candidate Bettina Jarasch voiced her support for the expropriation of the housing companies whose large shareholder payouts had been funded by sharp increases in rental income. But at the national level, the Greens continued to rule out expropriation, arguing instead that a rent cap might be the better solution. Nonetheless, 56.4 per cent of Berliners said 'Yes' to the expropriation of up to 240,000 units that could finally be returned to public ownership. (Many flats were constructed and paid for by the city before coming into private ownership.) And while the referendum is not yet legally binding – it must first be passed as a bill by the city council – this is still a small victory. Yet it is also true that the bill will probably never be passed: the SPD's Franziska Giffey – a staunch social conservative and favourite for the position of Berlin mayor – has already said that she would do everything in her power to prevent an expropriation of major landlords. The FDP, CDU/CSU and AfD hold the same position. Jarasch voted 'yes' in the referendum, but insists that expropriation is only a 'last resort'. And, more concerning: more than half of Berliner's voted for expropriation, but only 11.4 per cent voted for Die Linke.

Many Germans seem to have little faith in Die Linke. Despite a good programme and strong public performances by Kipping and Wissler – less so by Hennig-Wellsow who couldn't name where the *Bundeswehr* (German troops) were stationed – in the run up to the election, the party was unable to mobilise voters. Even Kipping, whose campaign in Saxony's Dresden 1 constituency sought to prevent a direct mandate for the AfD candidate, Jens Maier, only finished second behind the CDU's Markus Reichel. And the party's last-ditch attempt to pitch itself as a bulwark against a traffic light coalition of SPD, Greens and FDP wasn't well received by either its traditional base or young leftists in Germany's cities. It is difficult not to agree with Balhorn's assessment that Die Linke has lost touch with both its traditional base in the East and younger voters across the country who perceive 'the "hip" subcultural aesthetic the party has tried to lend its public image in recent years [as] forced'. Of course, paying lip service to social movements such as Fridays for Future or BlackLivesMatter is not enough to win an election; but it remains the case that the populist project of winning back voters by mimicking far-right rhetoric about immigration or a left-behind (left) working class – as Wagenknecht and Aufstehen attempted to do in 2018 – cannot be a desirable strategy for the left. In any case, Die Linke did not look like a party ready to govern; and it is unlikely that it will be anytime soon.

Instead, the SPD not only benefited from disappointed CDU voters who could no longer envision Laschet as a viable successor to Merkel, but also from Die Linke's decline: since the last election in 2017, 820,000 voters have abandoned the left and given their support to the Social Democrats. While some have sought to explain this phenomenon by pointing to the SPD's new leadership – Saskia Esken and Norbert Walter-Borjans are situated considerably further left than Scholz – and the leftward push of the Jusos (Working Group of Youth Socialists in the SPD) led by the outspoken Kevin Kühnert, their impact has been limited: when the new leadership duo of Esken and Walter-Borjans was elected in December 2019, the SPD was still polling between 14 and 17 per cent. What, then, can explain the exodus of voters from the left? Of course, the SPD benefited significantly from Die Linke's factional infighting and its inability to run a convincing campaign. But in the end, it was Scholz who made all the difference: the seasoned politician who has held the posts of General Secretary of the SPD, mayor of Hamburg, finance minister, labour minister and vice chancellor looked like the most reliable and stable candidate. Has the SPD, which has often been treated as a prime example of Pasokification (the decline of centre-left social democratic parties in Europe) finally found a way to avoid the fate of many of its European counterparts? And could a 'social, ecological, liberal' traffic light government of SPD, Greens and FDP really be a 'Petri dish for progressivism' as the *New Statesman*'s Jeremy Cliffe suggests?

The Darker Shades of Green

The idea that a traffic light coalition could lead to anything progressive seems far-fetched considering the last time the Greens and the SPD formed a national government. In an essay for *analyse & kritik*, writer and editor Sebastian Bähr explores the effects of the red-green coalition led by Gerhard Schröder on working people through an anecdote about a family holiday by the Baltic Sea. Throughout the holiday, Bähr's father is tormented by chronic pain and fatigue, and opts to stay inside or smoke on the balcony when the others are going out for walks. Bähr later explains that the long shift at the local supermarket – his father started working at the supermarket after losing his job in a combine harvester factory after reunification, when the GDR's struggling industrial sector finally collapsed – are to blame for his father's deteriorating health. At first, the supermarket job provided the family with relative comfort and stability (at the expense of any kind of personal fulfilment, Bähr notes). But things took a turn for the worse under the red-green government (SPD and Greens) in the early 2000s: as part of the Agenda 2010, the Schröder government abolished collective bargaining agreements in the retail sector, encouraging supermarkets to lower wage costs in order to stay competitive. As working hours became less regulated, overtime became the norm and shifts became more and more exhausting. And without proper union representation or other forms of labour protection, retail workers were left to fend for themselves.

In 'Dreams and Nightmares of the World's Middle Classes', Göran Therborn identifies two interrelated reasons for the end of the social-corporatist pact, explaining that

> [the] end of the working-class century had an economic
> basis in the accelerating deindustrialization and
> financialization of the capitalist core; more obliquely, a
> sociological factor was the social dissolution stemming
> from the 1968 cultural movement.

The decline of traditional Social Democracy was accompanied by a corresponding loss of social status for traditional working and middle class Germans. But it also led to the emergence of a new middle class whose influence increased as industrial and physical work lost its social status and the knowledge economy began to emerge, bringing with it a low-wage service sector. This is all well-known. But Bähr's essay doesn't just rehash the story of the decline of Social Democracy, as many have already done. Instead, it points to the difficulty that he and his parents have communicating about the things that exhaust and oppress them. They are missing a shared vocabulary, and when it comes to figuring out who might best represent their interests on the left, both are at a loss. Bähr sees his own predicament as symptomatic of a cultural left that has lost touch with working-class concerns. His parents want organised structures of solidarity that could help them solve concrete problems, but Bähr and his generation cannot provide this. *All die klugen Bücher helfen mir hier nicht weiter* – all the clever, leftist books he knows and has read can't help him now.

While the category of the middle class has never really been stable, there is a consensus that it is somehow threatened or in decline in the global north. This narrative of downward mobility was, of course, fuelled by fears of job losses through automation and rising inequality due to the bourgeoisie's appropriation of ever larger shares of national income. But in purely economic terms, the middle class isn't as threatened as it is made out to be: since the mid-1980s, their share of national income in OECD countries has only decreased by 5 per cent. Rather, anxieties around cultural decline have played a more important role in furthering this narrative. As Therborn shows, the belief in a 'class being abandoned, left behind by a previously admired economic leadership and lifestyle model' is shared by most of what Andreas Reckwitz calls the 'old middle class': relatively well-off workers with mid-level education who tend to be socially conservative and live outside of Germany's major cities. After the disastrous 2017 elections, many had predicted that there would be an exodus of old middle class (and working class) voters from the SPD. But the 2021 election has shown that the party is still capable of recapturing parts of its base, especially those who had drifted left to Die Like or right to the AfD. Parts of 'new middle class' – urban, educated and (self-identifyingly) progressive – have instead found a home in the Greens, whose MPs have represented their interests since the party's inception.

When the Greens formed a coalition with the SPD in 1998, there was little left of the anti-nuclear power and anti-war party that had emerged on the political scene in the wake of 1968. As Joachim Jachnow explains in 'What's Become of the German Greens' – perhaps the best summary of the party's history available in English – the Greens started out as a loose umbrella organisation for citizen's action groups (*Bürgerinitiativen*) who opposed the SPD's nuclear power programme and the social conservatism of the Helmut Schmidt government. At first, there was little need to participate in the sort of parliamentarism that many of the groups rejected. Moreover, the decentralised and anti-authoritarian character of the action groups had made it difficult to form a coherent party. Soon, however, Greens were standing in local elections and the party grew rapidly in numbers. And as the party grew, so did the different factions that were united under its banner: at one point, the Greens included Maoists, pacifists, individual anarchists and squatters, eco-libertarians and socially conservative environmentalists. But a commitment to environmental and anti-nuclear energy activism could not hold the party together: as Realos (reformists) like Fisher and Daniel Cohn-Bendit – former comrades in Frankfurt's squatting milieu – increasingly drifted to the right and positioned themselves as establishment politicians, other factions emerged including the radical ecologists (Fundis), eco-socialists and eco-libertarians, all of whom vehemently disagreed on the question of parliamentary strategy.

As the Greens steadily improved their electoral results – owing to the success of its reformist politics – the Realos continued to gain strength, and eco-socialists and other radicals were sidelined. When the party was finally forced to address the question of governing with the SPD following the state election in Hesse in 1983, conflicts that had been brewing for years finally came to the surface. For the radical left Fundis, the coalition agreement was nothing less than a betrayal of the party's anti-establishment principles; but for Fisher and Cohn-Bendit a coalition with the SPD was an opportunity to change the system from within. The Realos eventually managed to sideline the Fundis, and force prominent leftists such as Rainer Trampert, Thomas Ebermann and Julia Ditfurth out of the party in the late 1980s. With Fischer as the first state minister for the environment, Jachnow writes:

> The party proceeded to break every pledge it had ever made, including allowing nuclear plants to continue at full blast after the explosion at Chernobyl, flatly against the Greens' official position.

While Fischer was eventually sacked by the SPD's Holger Börner, the Greens continued to gain electoral ground, winning 8.3 per cent at the next federal elections in 1987. And while most of the party membership 'still voted for a radical agenda at Green assemblies, the parliamentary faction – dominated by reformists – tacitly ignored them, until the party finally gave way'.

When *Realsozialismus* (actually-existing socialism) began to collapse in the GDR, the West German Greens were already firmly embedded in the parliamentary system. And as reunification became more likely, the party was split over what position to take. While the party membership had initially opposed reunification because it would enable German military aggression abroad; have disastrous consequences for the East German economy; and lead to the re-emergence of the ethno-nationalist fantasy of a German *Volk* (peoples), underprepared West German Greens MPs eventually supported the move. As the party absorbed East German Greens and Bündnis 90 – a party made up of liberal civil and human rights groups who had opposed the rule of the SED (Socialist Unity Party) – its transformation into a national political party was complete. After reunification, the Greens shifted even further to the right, as the Realos formed an alliance with other eco-libertarians who shared their enthusiasm for market-based solutions to ecological issues. This was the final straw for many leftists, who finally decided to leave the party. Once the Greens joined the Schröder government, it became clear just how comfortable their MPs were as part of the political establishment. By now the Greens had become 'the most reliably Atlanticist of Germany's parties', supporting the NATO bombing of Serbia and the deployment of German troops to Afghanistan.

Jachnow concludes his *New Left Review* essay from 2013 by arguing that the 'Greens have paid strikingly little for their political mutation'; and despite the party's relatively disappointing performance in the election, this is still true today. For the first time since 2005 – the end of the Schröder government and the beginning of the Merkel era – the Greens will be part of a national government. And the party, which has done little to distance itself from its metropolitan, neoliberal image, has achieved this without appealing to voters outside of its urban middle class base in West German cities. Like the FDP, the Greens positioned themselves as a future-oriented party of the new middle class. And considering the relative strength and influence of this class, it is likely that both parties will continue to play key roles as power brokers in future elections. But what next for the Greens? As Baerbock has moved out of the spotlight, Robert Habeck – Fischer's preferred candidate – has stepped up to handle coalition negotiations. How many of their campaign pledges the Greens will have to sacrifice remains to be seen; but it is certain that dealing with the social, economic and ecological crises that Merkel leaves behind will be difficult for any coalition government.

The Limits of Eco-Merkelism

A week before the election, the *Economist* ran an editorial titled 'The mess Merkel leaves behind' unfavourably comparing Merkel's tenure as chancellor with that of Germany's longest-running head of state, Otto von Bismarck, and its longest-running chancellor, Helmut Kohl. (Merkel started her career in the CDU as Kohl's protégé). While Bismarck is, of course, best known for masterminding the unification of Germany and implementing the first embryonic welfare state, Kohl's legacy is a little shakier: while he did oversee the reunification of East and West Germany, he also led Germany into the Euro, which has so far been to the country's benefit but which might no longer continue to be so. What will Merkel's legacy be? In her sixteen-year tenure as chancellor, Merkel has solidified Germany's role within the EU, overseen a period of continuous growth – enabled by Schröder's labour market reforms – and crafted an image as a liberal, open and truly European leader. As the *Financial Times* put it, 'Merkel has established herself as Europe's pre-eminent stateswoman, a rock of stability in a world convulsed by economic crises, political populism and the fracturing of old alliances'. But stability has come at the cost of complacency; and the elections confirmed just how little imagination Germans have when choosing their next government. What most are looking for, really, is more of the same.

But as industry declines, economic growth stagnates and inflation rises, cracks in the state (and society) that Merkel is leaving behind are starting to show. According to the 2021 Annual Economic Report by the Federal Ministry for Economic Affairs and Energy, the German economy has 'entered its most severe recession for decades. With GDP falling by over 5 per cent in 2020 and massive public spending required to bolster the long-term fallout from the pandemic, the country's next government is backed into a corner on the question of the debt brake. While the coronavirus crisis has pushed Germany towards its first fiscal deficit in nearly a decade – the Federal Office for Statistics estimates that the government spent

€139.6 billion more than its revenue during 2020, which amounts to a deficit of 4.2 per cent of GDP – it would be wrong to conclude that Germany's next finance minister should once again insist on the *Schwarze Null* (balanced budgets) and the debt brake. The Kfw, a state-owned investment and development bank, has warned that there is an investment backlog of €149 billion. Yet as social infrastructure crumbles, politicians continue to promote orthodox ordoliberal fiscal policy. It would take a two-thirds majority in parliament to change the constitution, so it will be difficult for the Greens, for example, to push through their proposed €500 billion digital and climate focused public investment programme.

Keeping the debt brake will also have knock on effects for Germany's role in Europe. As Streeck points out in 'Will it Be Enough?'

> German national debt [has] increased in 2020 from 60 per cent to 70 per cent of GDP, and is likely to increase at the same pace, to about 80 per cent. There are no indications that Germany's next government, regardless of its composition, would be able, or indeed willing, to abolish the so called 'debt brake' written into the constitution in 2009, meaning that fiscal policy in coming years will still have to observe narrow limits on borrowing. [...] Moreover, already before the pandemic, German public infrastructure – roads, bridges, the railway system – had noticeably decayed over the past two decades, due not least to the self-imposed austerity, intended to teach other EU member states that saving must precede spending. Now Corona has drawn attention to further deficiencies in healthcare, nursing homes, schools and universities, all of which will be expensive to re-dress.

What this means, is that there is little space in the budget for further payments to weaker EU member states. (Germany accounts for over 20 per cent of the bloc's GDP and contributes around €17.2

billion more than it receives). If payments continue, Streeck argues, this could lead to discontent at home, which neither the SPD, Greens or FDP are equipped to deal with. Under Merkel, Germany has suppressed domestic demand and forced austerity in weaker member states, while maintaining the Euro as a sort of devalued Deutschmark. (Without the Euro, a strong Deutschmark would undermine Germany's trade advantage and make it more difficult to maintain a surplus). Whether the joint borrowing scheme for the post-pandemic recovery fund and the offer of grants instead of loans to indebted Southern states means that the 'ordoliberalisation of the EU has stalled' as Boris Frankel suggests remains to be seen. But it is certain that Germany will continue to pursue its national interest in the Union.

Michael Roberts has argued that German capitalism has been successful for three reasons. First, it was able to use the 'expansion of the European Union to relocate its key sectors into cheaper wage areas' in Southern and Eastern Europe. Second, Germany benefited from the introduction of the Euro through which it gained trade advantages. And third, the Hartz labour market reforms 'created a dual wage system that kept millions of workers on low pay as part-time temporary employees'. While Merkel has done much to build on these pillars, they are not of her own making: she inherited the European Monetary Union from Kohl; the Hartz labour-market reforms from Schröder; and the 'German system of industrial relations' (*Sozialpartnerschaft*) from earlier post-war governments. While the SPD paid dearly for the Agenda 2010 at the ballots – its vote share in the 2009 election fell from 34.2 to 23 per cent – Merkel continued to thrive, owing largely to the economic boost from trade advantages made possible by what, for Germany, is an undervalued Euro. But the pillars of the economy do not look as robust as they have in the past. Scholz's electoral success was built on the promise of lower inequality, higher wages, improvements in public services and infrastructure and higher taxes on the wealthiest Germans. This means that the Hartz labour market reforms cannot continue in their current form (though Lindner and the FDP will want to keep them in place). Moreover, the EU is beginning to look shakier than ever, as countries such as Poland – a major benefactor of EU transfers – retreat into a narrow nationalism, questioning how much they really benefit from the current arrangement. Holding the Union together while maintaining Germany's privileged role within it now seems like an impossible task.

In early September, the automobile industry gathered in Munich to attend the international mobility show, IAA (*Internationale Automobil-Ausstellung*). Under the banner of 'what will move us next?', executives and automobile enthusiasts discussed the future of global mobility focusing, of course, on auto-mobility alone and not on the expansion of public transport or the phasing out of private car ownership. During the week-long expo, there was a constant sound of helicopters and police sirens in the usually quiet city, as protests by environmental activists were violently broken up by police. And all this was taking place in the very city where the Greens achieved some of their best results (around 26 per cent in all three constituencies). In the end, it seems, the automobile industry still had the final say. This is not surprising considering the role it plays in the German economy: carmakers and their suppliers make up almost 10 per cent of GDP and over 930,000 people are employed in the sector. In 2020, cars or car parts made up 15.6 per cent of exports with an estimated value of over €187.5 billion. The general decline in industry has been much slower in Germany than in other European countries, with manufacturing still accounting for 23 per cent of Germany's national output (compared to a much lower 12 per cent in the United States and 10 per cent in the United Kingdom). So, with a crisis on the horizon, Germany is looking to its most prominent and reliable industrial sector as a lifeline.

Yet the sector has been hard hit by the coronavirus crisis and technological changes in car manufacturing which have seen US companies like Tesla surpass BMW and VW in the realm of electro mobility. Car-part manufacturers are being forced to shut their doors as their parts are no longer needed for battery-powered cars:

as Deutsche Welle reports, Bosch will cut thousands of jobs while Continental will try to save €1 billion each year by laying off 13,000 workers. Though the Boston Consulting Group estimates that there will be no net job losses by 2030, there will have to be significant (and expensive) reskilling of workers and a switch to lithium-ion battery production which will require building several new plants in the next eight years. It is no wonder, then, that even the Greens are cautious in their assessment of how long it will take to phase out the internal combustion engine. Moreover, an acute shortage of raw materials in Germany's industrial sector has shed light on the supply chains the auto industry relies on to keep production going. As bottlenecks plague global supply chains and energy prices continue to rise – the current shortage in semiconductors is an example – Germany is becoming more and more aware of how vulnerable it is to such disruptions. And with rising energy prices leading to inflation, workers and unions have started to demand higher wages – a problem for an economy that relies on keeping wages relatively low to maintain export competitiveness.

International trade might also prove more difficult for German manufacturers moving forward. For the past five years, Germany's main trade partner has been China. (While Germany still exports most of its goods to the US, the overall trade volume with China is much larger: in 2020, traded goods amounted to €212.9 billion, compared to €171.5 with the United States.) As the Chinese economy slows down and the US and other strategic (NATO) partners impose further sanctions as part of a hawkish geopolitical approach to the 'threat of China' this is likely to cause problems. Last year's EU-China investment treaty is yet to be ratified by the European Parliament and the Greens, who subscribe to the NATO stance on China, are unlikely to help push through the deal Merkel put in place. Moreover, Chinese electric vehicle (EV) manufacturers are considering building assembly plants in Europe and seeking export markets abroad. While none of the Chinese manufacturers can really compete with the likes of VW, this is still an important shift: China is the world's largest car market and any loss of market share could hurt Germany's economy. (VW has unveiled plans to cut 30,000 jobs and argued that the company needed to 'address the competitiveness [...] in view of new market entrants', though it has just paid out €2.4 billion in dividends and made a profit of around €8.8 billion). Germany's export-oriented industrial sector isn't looking quite as robust as it did during Merkel's tenure.

So what role will, or can, Germany's next government play in enabling the social and economic transformation so desperately needed to address the climate crisis? Above all, the Merkel era provided a bulwark against any sort of social-ecological transformation. And the eco-Merkelism proposed by a traffic light coalition will surely mean more of the same, as Germany continues to externalise socio-ecological costs of increased production and capital accumulation. As Ulrich Brand and Markus Wissen argue in *The Imperial Mode of Living*, the fact that the demand for SUVs has gone up among more 'environmentally conscious' sections of the middle and upper-middle class points to contradictions in the 'green capitalism' that the Greens championed in their manifesto. Sure, there are ecological advantages offered by the operation of electric cars; but we must also take the ecological cost of their production into account.

As Brand and Wissen write:

> Oil is the fuel of fossil fuel-based automobility, but it is far from the only prerequisite. Before oil is used in a combustion engine, the latter must be constructed. The same goes for the chassis, undercarriage, transmission, electronic system and interior of the vehicle. Raw materials are used in all of these components, materials that follow complex and destructive paths on their way to the final product, whose use they make possible. The most important raw materials such as iron, aluminium and copper.

Where does the auto industry source these materials? 56 per cent of iron ore imported into the country comes from Brazil, and the rest from China and Australia; no iron ore has been mined on German soil since 1987 and all demand is met by imports. Lithium for the batteries that Germany plans on producing locally, will most likely come from Bolivia, Zimbabwe, Chile, Australia or China. And while there are still enough lithium reserves to meet increased production of batteries, platinum and copper are much rarer and production might not be able to keep up with demand. Of course, the mining of both raw materials will have devastating ecological consequences.

IG Metall – Germany's largest union with a membership of around 2.27 million – is an enthusiastic supporter of electro-mobility. Yet the union refuses to recognise that, in the long run, the transition to electric vehicles will not benefit German workers but rather car manufacturers, who can increase their profits as people are forced to scrap or sell their old cars and buy new ones. The EV transition doesn't look too great for the environment either: as long-time VW worker Lars Hirsekorn points out, the production of a standard (electric) Golf, for example, emits 8.5 tonnes of CO_2. Moreover, there is a dire need for reskilling workers to prepare them for a 'greener' economy, but IG Metall has done little to prepare its members. As layoffs become more frequent in the auto industry, the union has, of course, sought to protect the jobs of its members. The problem here, Hirsekorn argues, is that IG Metall didn't support their comrades working in public transport (and represented by Germany's second largest union, ver.di) when they were striking for better pay, even though this is precisely the kind of industry that might employ former automobile workers if there is a green transition.

Like most German unions, IG Metall represents only a limited section of what Lenin called the labour aristocracy. Unsurprisingly, it has continued to neglect the demands of migrant and agency workers – a large section of Germany's working class. The post-war model of industrial citizenship relied on the notion of the white, male worker i.e., the family breadwinner whose interests (and by extension those of his family) were represented by the union.

But women and migrant workers fell outside the remit of union bargaining. The result was a two-tiered labour system in which workers who perform the same tasks are paid vastly different wages under worse working conditions. Historically, this has had disastrous consequences for workplace organising: in 1973, for example, when migrant workers launched a wildcat strike to fight against the termination of 300 Turkish workers without notice, the union IG Metall refused to back the strike; and to make matters worse, most German workers didn't join their comrades at the picket line. The practice of separating union-represented workers from migrant and agency workers has continued to define the German economy, with unions playing a major role in maintaining this system. There is little reason to have faith in the radical potential of the country's exclusive and archaic union bureaucracy.

The wildcat strike at the grocery delivery service Gorillas is a case in point. In response to the unlawful firing of a colleague, the company's riders united under the banner of the Gorillas Workers Collective (GWC) to demand better working conditions, higher wages and secure employment. But unions were reluctant to support strike action that could be illegal; and though the wildcat strike was the only method available to the riders, ver.di deemed it too radical to endorse. In many ways, ver.di's response was characteristic of Germany's outdated unions, who still seem to believe that their sole purpose is to negotiate collective bargaining agreements. But the traditional methods of industrial relations are not suited to the situation of precariously employed (and often migrant) workers. While the GWC has now elected a works council to arrange a collective bargaining agreement with their employer, many riders still fear that union involvement will mean a loss of control, as unions take over and de-radicalise the strike to further their own interests. At Gorillas, 350 workers lost their jobs and the unions did little to prevent this. Clearly, unions such as ver.di or IG Metall aren't the unproblematic vehicles of the working class struggle they are sometimes made out to be.

As Germany enters the next phase of Merkelism (without Merkel) – it is likely that only a few will benefit from the limited transition to a greener economy. Migrant and agency workers will continue to be employed at below minimum wage; indigenous communities in mining towns will continue to shoulder the burden of the intensified mining required for the transition to electro-mobility; and emissions will continue to be externalised to countries (socially and economically) less able to meet the arbitrary climate targets that the developed economies of the global north have set themselves. But the ideals of social stability and economic growth that Germans have become attached to are coming up against their ecological limits. There is dire need for popular mobilisation for a radical ecological programme, a nationalisation of key industries and a concept of global worker's solidarity. But the imperial mode of living is hard-wired into German society and change is unlikely to come from anywhere within the country's parliamentary system. What next?

What is needed is the kind of change that the Salvage Collective has described as 'farther reaching and deeper in its action, than the Renaissance, or the Enlightenment, or the bourgeois-democratic revolutions, or the colonial freedom movement'. In short, we need a new communism. Yet the best outcome we can currently hope for is the kind of 'communism' the right has conjured as a straw-man – a timid 'communism' which looks a lot like a 'greener' Social Democracy. This will not suffice to repair lives or salvage ecosystems that have been devastated by capital accumulation. There is much to be done to make the unthinkable real; the left still has a role to play.

TAD DELAY

Denial Futures

'You're not from around here, are you?'

It is autumn 2020. Wildfires stretching the West Coast paint the skies burnt orange. In various places the hue at noon is blood red. Five of the largest ten wildfires in Californian history burn simultaneously.

Nobody alive has witnessed such ruin. It has not been so hot since the Eemian interglacial period some 130,000 years ago, when temperatures averaged under a degree warmer, driving our ancestors out of Africa while seas rose a metre every twenty years for several centuries. Between the origins of agriculture along the Tigris and Euphrates to the invention of hydraulic fracturing, indeed in the entire history of civilisation after we left the cave, it has never been so hot. But paleoclimate data is not on the mind of the vigilante barking, 'You're not from around here, are you?'

He is armed. He points his question at an African-American mother fleeing wildfires. She registers the racial overtones of the inquisition.

She's stopped at an improvised checkpoint in Corbett, Oregon. Fires threaten communities around Portland, an overwhelmingly white area of the Pacific Northwest. Evacuees take to the roads.

It is the year of the pandemic, after a summer of mass protests for racial justice in the wake of murders by police. An election approaches; the incumbent praises violence. Police assault countless citizens. Over a hundred reactionaries ram protestors with vehicles; conservative legislatures rush through bills to authorise the manslaughter tactic. Hundreds of thousands die of a virus. America is about to erupt, wallowing in a desire for – what? Not a desire to know anything.

'You're not from around here, are you?'

His eyes dart from her to the other occupants, scanning the vehicle and gauging threats. In the back, her young children stare back at the vigilante and the weapon with which he might dispatch them. No, these are not the targets. He is searching for arsonists, saboteurs, the Right's hallucinated fixation: antifa.

In nearby Estacada, a journalist is accosted and flees. As he speeds away, a truck intercepts from the front, blocking the highway. Out of the vehicle emerges a gunman aiming his rifle through the journalist's windshield.

A few miles southwest in Mollala, three journalists are stopped at another improvised checkpoint, guns raised. A vigilante snaps, 'Get the fuck out of here', as he takes photos of their faces and license plate.

'It seems like the militants are burning out/up the rural folks closest to the cities', says one member of a Facebook group organising the counterattack, 'because the only way they can fight is dirty vs the more conservative/rural folks would hand them their @$$es [sic] in an altercation.' Another suggests they fight. 'Most of us can mobilize and bring our arsenal with us.' The radio reports antifa shooting at firefighters.

Police are alerted to illegal checkpoints but do not intervene. After a school board member organises citizen patrols, a sheriff's sergeant asks for 'photos of cars and even license plates'. He advises vigilantes watch out for 'anything that feels out of place to you, just listen to your gut because nine times out of ten your gut is right'.

A Clackamas County sheriff's deputy is forced out of his job after a video goes viral in which he erupts at the imaginary culprits. 'What I'm worried about is that there's people stashing stuff. It means that they're gonna go in preparation. And I don't wanna sound like some doomsdayer, but it's getting serious, and, I, we need the public's help on this'.

Another interjects to say people around Portland will simply stay home and die in the inferno rather than risk evacuating only to encounter anarchists. The deputy blurts, 'Antifa motherfuckers, okay, are out causing hell. And there's a lot of lives at stake, and there's a lot of people's property at stake, because these guys got some vendetta.'

The next day, this same deputy advises a citizen's group they must be cautious when using deadly force. When they kill outsiders, he tells them, the courts will demand explanation. He laughs with them, charming the bloodthirsty piglets. 'Now, you throw a fucking knife in their hand after you shoot 'em, that's on you.' More laughter from the crowd. He assures them, 'I am on your side, people, I am one hundred percent! I wouldn't let this shit happen in my neighborhood either, but be smart about it.'

Over a weekend in September 2020, illegal checkpoints and armed squads spring up independently in at least three towns near Portland. Fueled on social media rumors and encouraged by police, citizens organically convert latent climate denial, scouting instead for imaginary leftists while pointing weapons at reporters and families. Thankfully there are no reports of lethal violence this time. A near miss. You're not from around here, are you?

We are, all of us, in denial about what awaits us in the Changes. Not just the conservatives. Liberals and social democrats deny as well; so too does the Left.

Denial is repression, the putting away of an unpleasant idea. We deny because we are human. We repress. Repression and the return of the repressed are the same. What cannot be confronted converts into stranger commitments and violence.

The easiest path of denial ignores the problem *tout court*, but denial takes active paths as well. Freud said denial allows the subject to accept what is repressed without disturbing the repressions. 'You ask who this person in the dream can be', his patient would say. 'It's not my mother.' Freud translated negations as, 'This is something which I should prefer to repress.'

Patients expressed two denials, Freud said. One denial tried escaping moral judgment. The other simply denied reality itself.

With climate change, the conservative denies reality. We mock them for it, but that's such low-hanging fruit. On the other hand, the liberal who cries 'Believe the science!' seeks to escape guilt, vehemently lashing out against what needs to be done. If we need to decarbonise the economy and dislodge capitalism, the liberal says we must be more pragmatic. If the only candidate to propose a marginally decent climate plan is a socialist, the liberal suddenly remembers climate change is not so important. The moralising confesses: this is something that I should prefer to repress.

Moralising is obnoxious but also dangerous. This isn't a game. Don't you see what's on the horizon?

It is the late winter of 2020. Greece announces a plan to erect nets in the Aegean Sea. There are too many Syrians. They flee a civil war resulting from displaced people concentrating in hot cities during a drought. The nets will have flashing lights and rise half a metre out of the water, either to catch or drown Syrians. The crisis owes itself to a warmer climate. Nets don't discriminate.

It is 1978. Exxon scientists discuss the greenhouse effect and predict the Western Antarctic ice sheet's collapse. Internal reports soon speak of widespread disaster, including a multimetre sea level rise and the flooding of Florida and Washington DC. An alerted public might force them to strand assets and shutter operations. Exxon launches a misinformation campaign nearly a decade before the public learns the term 'global warming'.

It is November 2018. A future United States congressperson

announces on Facebook her investigation into wildfires. 'There are too many coincidences to ignore', she smartly hints. Democrats and Jewish bankers, she says, are colluding to clear the countryside for high speed trains. They are using satellite platforms to beam solar radiation into the forest. 'Could that cause a fire?' she asks of culprits she's outed. 'Hmmm, I don't know.' Once more blaming liberals and Jews for space lasers rather than climate change, she feigns humility. 'But what do I know? I just like to read a lot.'

It is anytime in the so-called War on Terror. Drones strike wedding parties and school buses, and occasionally they hit a militant resisting imperialists. Regions hit lie on the aridity line, the liminal zone where barely enough rain falls for crops, winding from the African Sahel through the Middle East. The United States and its allies carry out drone strikes along the aridity line in Mali, Libya, Yemen, Sudan, Somalia, Niger, Iraq, Afghanistan, and Syria. European policies of externalising borders redirect northbound African migrants eastward into neighbouring states, hoping refugees get bogged down and remain in Africa. Heat-stressed and drought-stricken areas pack tighter still. Some rebel. Those who do are labelled terrorists and slated for termination. All for lack of rainfall on an aridity line that is, thanks to warming, moving year by year. Plot the advance of desertification, and one might see where drones will soon lurk. Meanwhile, Westerners nervously whisper of approaching water wars, as if we are not already engaged.

It is the now and the near future. Bangladesh's Kutupalong camp, the largest refugee camp in the world, is critically full with Rohingya driven out of Myanmar. The location is vulnerable to cyclones and flooding. The government relocates a substantial portion of the population from the current camp in Cox's Bazar to an island called Bhasan Char. The low-lying island is not twenty years old, formed from silt from the Meghna River. Already, at high tide in a storm the island could be submerged – even before the seas rise, that is. Authorities will move hundreds of thousands of refugees to an island which will be drowned.

The conversion symptoms proliferate.

Ɠ

Conflicts in the psyche often manifest in the body. This is no longer controversial. One need not be a psychoanalyst to see it; so-called cognitive or evidence-based psychologies say the same thing. But psychoanalysts discovered it as early as they discovered the talking cure.

The conversion symptom is a very old idea worth a hearing again. Freud and his colleague Joseph Breuer studied how the latter's patient, Anna O, suffered physical symptoms from psychic stress. She dreamt a snake attacked her father, and ever after the sight of a snake caused her arm to stiffen. Her anxiety robbed her of the ability to speak her native tongue, yet she retained use of English. These are conversion symptoms.

The conversion symptom is a return of the repressed, from the psyche to the body. Psychoanalyst Bruce Fink listed 'minor aches and pains, tightness in the chest, a tingling sensation, a burning sensation, and dizziness to migraines, paralysis, blindness, muteness, and deafness'. Today those resistant to psychoanalytic thought still complain of stress-related irritable bowel disorder.

Of what am I trying to warn? In its protean vectors, climate change and its often violent denial are, in a manner of speaking, conversion symptoms of capitalism's inability to deal with a carbon dependency.

People speak of capitalism as if it's an incidental roadblock obstructing climate mitigation, in the same way conservative and liberal parties slow necessary steps. But this misrepresents the relationship. No, capitalism is not a roadblock: capitalism is the generator. The tendency of profit to follow the path of highest return, the pressure to lure investors with ever-greater profits quarter after quarter, the praise for unlimited expansion in a world of finite resources, labour exploitation and destruction of nature, the allure of cheap energy no matter the cost, and most of all the ability to discount true ecological and social costs which don't show up yet in the exchange value – in such a deranged machine, climate change is a conversion disorder of capitalism.

If climate change is a conversion disorder of capital, other conversion symptoms follow in denial. 'It is not the consciousness of men that determines their existence', as Marx said of the hazy awareness we build burning carbon, 'but, on the contrary, their social existence determines their consciousness.' In the nineties, ExxonMobil paid the *New York Times* to sow doubt about the human causes a full generation after its own sciences proved anthropogenic warming in the late seventies. In the aughts, BP instructed consumers to fret about a new marketing gimmick called a carbon footprint. In the West, politicians brag of the stock market's growth and energy independence in the same breath as emissions targets. Senator Elizabeth Warren campaigns on greening the military. Bill Gates brags of purchasing sustainable jet fuel for his private gallivanting. Pundits speak of 'fighting' climate change without specifics. The Paris Climate Agreement pretends there is hope for remaining below 1.5°C via non-binding pledges projected to push us over 3°C.

Indeed, the symptoms proliferate. We see them everywhere.

It is September 2018. Buried in a five-hundred-page report by the National Highway Traffic Safety Administration is a proposal to roll back Obama-era regulations on vehicle emissions. The agency acknowledges global temperatures will increase 3.5°C by 2100. What stands out, though, is not so much an agency housed within the executive branch of a climate denier acknowledging mainstream consensus. No, what stuns in an otherwise dry report is a plan to raise temperatures and sea levels further.

'The amazing thing they're saying is human activities are going to lead to this rise of carbon dioxide that is disastrous for the environment and society', explains Michael MacCracken, a senior climate scientist. 'And then they're saying they're not going to do anything about it.' Old regulations cost money. Warming is inevitable. Better to relax standards and reap rewards today. A machine which cannot think more than a few financial quarters ahead need not worry for the grandchildren of the ghouls reaping rewards now.

Do you want to know why we won't be limiting warming to that ambitious Paris Agreement goal of 1.5°C or 2°C? Let me show you the math for denial futures.

A carbon budget is used to estimate how much CO_2 we can still burn before surpassing a temperature threshold, usually given as 1.5°C or 2°C warming by 2100. Budgets are measured in gigatonnes of carbon dioxide ($GtCO_2$). In 2018, the Intergovernmental Panel on Climate Change set a budget of 420 $GtCO_2$ to limit warming to 1.5°C above pre-industrial temperatures. To limit warming to 2°C, the budget was 1,170 $GtCO_2$.

We emit 42 $GtCO_2$ per year, so subtract three years to get a remaining budget of 294 $GtCO_2$ for limiting to 1.5°C, and 1,044 for 2°C. The uncertainty is ±400 Gt CO_2, so we might have locked in 1.5°C warming even if all emissions ceased today. Fine.

Nobody has an intuitive grasp of what it means to sequester so much carbon. Unfortunately, we have a recent example of winding down emissions. The historic lockdown measures put in place to slow the spread of Covid-19 dropped emissions 2.4 $GtCO_2$ in 2020. Do the maths. The Covid-19 shutdown postponed the apocalyptic threshold by a couple of weeks.

Next, add up reserves of fossil fuels – raw materials, current prices, and carbon dioxide content if burned – in order to see the total cost in dollars and carbon dioxide. Not all crude oil and natural gas is burned, since plastics and lubricants are derived from fossil fuels, but the vast majority is burned. While psychotic energy markets fret over the need to diversify with clean energy for the sake of strong portfolios, the problem is precisely that exhausting non-renewables is so profitable.

Crude oil's energy return on investment remains high, slightly outperforming the efficiency of photovoltaic solar. Other renewables such as hydroelectric and wind power vastly outperform all fossil fuels, but they require massive investments. Instead, unconventional extraction techniques such as fracking pull fuel from tar sands with such energy-intensive methods that unconventionals hover just above or dip below the efficiency of burning wood. In fact, unconventional fuel sources provide such a low return on energy investment that they fall well below the minimum threshold of efficiency needed for modern civilisation.

How can that be? How can the supremely wise market – for now – invest in resources that aren't efficient enough to support civilisation? Because governments charged with protecting us are instead propping up fossil-fuel companies with subsidies, and even low efficiencies still yield profit; even without subsidies, half of new oil-extraction projects would still be profitable enough to continue. The energy return on investment of tar sands is, at most, only one thirtieth as efficient as the oil fields of the mid-nineteenth century. However fake the subsidised numbers, good fossil-fuel reports convert to happy markets, which convert to ghoulish campaign talking points, duped constituents, and threatened ecosystems.

If we burned all fossil fuels, clean-energy alternatives would be a moot point, on account of locking in 9°C warming which would make food production impossible and raise oceans seventy metres.

The fossil-fuel industry keeps close track of reserves, which is their sole respectable contribution to my research interests. The following table is my own, derived from BP's surprisingly granular reporting on reserves, current fossil fuel prices, and Environmental Protection Agency conversions for CO_2 emitted from each source. These numbers are for reserves only, which are deposits profitably extractable with current technology; this does not even count fossil-fuel resources, which could become reserves if extraction technology improves or if government subsidies incentivise further exploration.

Conventional Crude
- Current market value: $107.5 trillion (1.73 trillion barrels at $62/barrel)
- 746 $GtCO_2$ emitted if burned

Unconventional Oil (primarily shale oil and tar sands)
- Unknown resource total, conservatively estimated 7 trillion barrels, 15 per cent of which are recoverable reserves: $68.3 trillion (1.05 trillion at $65/barrel)
- 514.8 $GtCO_2$ emitted if burned

Coal
- Current market value: $43 trillion (1.07 trillion tonnes at $40/tonne)
- 2,135 $GtCO_2$ emitted if burned

Natural Gas
- Current market value: $28 trillion (7 quadrillion cubic feet at $4/thousand cubic feet)
- 384 $GtCO_2$ emitted if burned

Assets to be Stranded in Compliance with IPCC Carbon Budget
- Value of conventional oil, coal, natural gas, and unconventional oil: $246.8 trillion
- Emissions potential of all fossil fuel reserves: 3,805 GtCO2
- Remaining carbon budget to stay under 2°C warming: 1,044 $GtCO_2$
- To meet 2°C limit, we need to leave 73 per cent of fuels in the ground, stranding assets worth $179 trillion
- Remaining carbon budget to stay under 1.5°C: 294 $GtCO_2$
- To meet 1.5°C goal, we need to leave 92 per cent of fuels in the ground, stranding assets worth $227 trillion

What's the upshot? We've emitted approximately 2,200 $GtCO_2$ since the Industrial Revolution, less than half of the carbon dioxide we'll emit this century if we burn all remaining reserves. To avoid 2°C warming, we must strand 73 per cent of all remaining fossil-fuel reserves, a loss of $179 trillion. If we wish to meet the more ambitious Paris Agreement goal of limiting warming to 1.5°C, we must strand 92 per cent of fossil fuels, a staggering loss of $227 trillion. Again, these numbers assume companies already walk away from an additional half quadrillion dollars in unconventional oil resources due to extraction trouble, so the reality might turn out worse.

Feel the gravity of this contradiction. This amount of money is almost certainly not collectable in full due to a range of factors, not the least of which would be economic lag from climate stress. The point of these numbers is to show the incentives today, which all point in the wrong direction. As much as 50 per cent of oil production is already unprofitable without government subsidies provided at the precise moment when higher prices could move the needle in the right direction. Cheap talk of vaguely 'fighting' climate change assumes states and companies, all of whom already claim these assets in their portfolios, will voluntarily walk away from mountains of cash. Even as cheaper renewables come online, everyone will want a piece of the remaining mountain. A trillion here, another trillion there.

We pretend finance austerity, the blowback of decoupling energy from carbon, can be accomplished within pseudo-democracies masking oligarchies, where craven policymakers fear withdrawn support from those who remember more lucrative times. Will the lords voluntarily walk away from hundreds of trillions of dollars without force? Who will force them?

It is a new millennium. British Petroleum rebrands, now using the lower case bp for 'beyond petroleum'. Nice. Unlike ExxonMobil's strategy of science denial, BP positions itself as the first green oil company. What a concept! Adopting a new logo of a sunburst in green, yellow, and white, they pioneer a field variously called environmental advertising, greenwashing, or green spin.

'What size is your carbon footprint?' asks black text in the ad blitz. Fade to interviews on the streets of London. 'Ah the carbon footprint, eh', one respondent pauses, 'that I don't know.' Another reframes the question, 'How much carbon I produce – is that it?' A final interviewee in Chicago rounds out the explanation. 'You mean the effect that my living has on the Earth in terms of the products I consume?' The ad fades back to white field, black text. 'We can all do more to emit less.'

BP launches a carbon footprint calculator in 2004 as a component of its green rebrand. The term enters the popular lexicon.

Louis Althusser drew two conclusions on ideology. First, ideology represents an imaginary relationship to real conditions, aiding in recognition and misrecognition (denial does the latter).

Secondly, ideology has a material existence. Ideology is housed within apparatuses, allowing people to act out and reproduce an ideology. Althusser listed a few ideological state apparatuses: the church or other religious institutions, schools, family, the legal system (which is both repressive and ideological), political parties, unions, media, literature, arts, sports, etc. That list was drafted a while ago. What apparatuses would we add today?

Visiting BP's calculator today, you will be offered an opportunity to purchase carbon offsets. Scant details about what counts as an offset hide among jargon about robust industry standards. What matters is, after adding your sins of emission, you may purchase an indulgence. How much would it cost to offset, say, 16 tonnes of carbon dioxide emissions, an annual average for an American? A mere seventy-two dollars.

> Wall Street now mirrors this scam for big investors. Blackrock CEO Larry Fink champions ESG (environmental, social, governance) investing. As Adrienne Buller explained in *Beyond the Ruins*, ESG investors and financial products buy shares

in companies (or their bonds) based on metrics purporting to measure their carbon emissions intensity, equitable labour practices, transparency, the diversity of their executive boards and so on … [T]he reality is somewhat different. To date, the ESG industry has established no rules for what counts as 'sustainable' or 'ethical'.

In fact, Buller noticed, Vanguard's flagship ESG fund invests in Apple, Amazon, Microsoft, Facebook, Google, and Tesla.

Travel a bit less, cut the carbon footprint. Recycle more. Stop flying. What's the floor? A study analysing various lifestyles, from children to monks to billionaires, found that the footprint of an American experiencing homelessness is still eight tonnes, roughly twice the global average. There's only so much one can do. BP would have you believe you can do more, though. Specifically, if we multiplied that fake seventy-two dollars by the number of consumers in America, they'd have us believe we can offset and fix the problem with a mere $24 billion per year. At the same time, investment groups looking to greenwash the petroleum in their portfolios eye ESGs, excusing bad Shell and ExxonMobil with good Amazon and Google.

If you critique these frauds, you will hear, 'Every little bit helps', and, 'Don't let the best be the enemy of the good.' What a deal when we feared we'd need to strand a quarter quadrillion! The symptoms proliferate, ever more stupid and violent.

It is 12 October 2018. Numbering one hundred and sixty, they set out from San Pedro Sula in Honduras. They track east through Guatemala and Mexico, then north to the US. In little more than a week, their ranks swell to as many as seven thousand. US media dubs it a 'migrant caravan'.

Some interpret the movement as a critique of a troubled Honduran government. Others say it is blowback from the coups, death squads, and genocides supported by the US in Honduras, Guatemala, El Salvador, and Nicaragua over the last half century. US VP Harris will later guess migrants are leaving Guatemala because of how it treats LGBT people and communities of colour.

The truth is, on top of imperialist violence, Central America is increasingly inhospitable to life. Guatemala, El Salvador, Honduras, and Nicaragua sit in the 'dry corridor', an area vulnerable to irregular rainfall. In the worst drought in four decades, more than a quarter do not have adequate money for food. 'If we are going to die anyway', said Honduran farmer Jorge Reyes in the anguish of hunger, 'we might as well die trying to get to the United States'.

The UN projects as many as a billion climate refugees displaced by 2050. Oxfam estimates 20 million refugees are already displaced annually by climate-change-fueled 'natural disasters', an antiquated term since disasters are no longer purely natural. The UN requests states recognise asylum requests due to climate disasters but does not make this demand binding; indeed, there is no legally binding category for 'climate refugee' or 'climate migrant', though such refugees outnumber war refugees by as many as ten to one.

On 16 October, President Trump tweets angrily for the first time about the caravan. Following up two days later, he inveighs, 'Sadly, it looks like Mexico's Police and Military are unable to stop the Caravan heading to the Southern Border of the United States. Criminals and unknown Middle Easterners are mixed in.' Rightwing media paints the families as ISIS insurgents.

Witness the future of denial in the resurrection of a long-dormant gimmick. After 9/11, the Department of Homeland Security was established with disingenuous claims that Al-Qaeda was pouring over the southern border. Now the president's mind, flickering in and out of timelines, resurrects the myth. White House Press Secretary Sarah Sanders lies that 4,000 terrorists were captured by border patrol in a year.

The President retweets an anti-semitic video claiming to show George Soros funding the caravan, Soros being a metonym for 'Jewish money' on the Right. Matt Gaetz also blames the caravan on Jewish money. Michael Savage says the caravan could signal 'the end of America as we know it'. Pat Buchanan warns, 'Yet far more critical to the future of our civilisation is the ongoing invasion of the West from the Third World.' A DHS spokesperson backs them up. Newt Gingrich joins in: 'If you were a terrorist and wanted to get in the United States and you saw 10,000 people trying to get into the United States, how unlikely is it that you might decide to join them?'

The caravan reaches the border. They request asylum. The US forces Mexico to settle those who don't return home. Their stories are harsh and tragic. They offer us a dazzling premonition about climate migration.

Today's inchoate or incipient fascisms, as Richard Seymour has rightly qualified this contested term, serve up a vision of the future. What will happen when hundreds of millions move, when the crops fail, when economies plummet? How long until the US and EU police their borders with armed drones, as Israel already does at the edge of Gaza? If the choice is socialism or barbarism, a fossil fascism will lash out nostalgically for a time before the seas swallowed the coasts while sneering at fleeing families: you're not from around here, are you?

'What was it like before the Changes?'

It is early in the twenty-second century. The old man doesn't know how to answer the kid's question. She knows too much. Her textbooks recall sand covering ground like this everywhere, on every coast of every sea in the world.

When he was her age he read up on the extinction of the rhinoceros. Of lower Manhattan's carbon-based traffic before the seawall ruptured. Los Angeles before the fires. Southern Europe before the nets and razor wire. The Sahel and Northern Triangle before the exodus. Oceans before the great dying. Bangladesh before the drowning. Her schoolbooks footnoted the last eagles or the first border sentry drones, sure, but the old man actually remembers things she reads like legends. The world is 4°C warmer.

They are sitting on a beach in northern Michigan. He is my

grandchild or yours, keeping watch over his family as best he can. The red sun sets over the lake. In the winter the waves still occasionally freeze like an eerie reminder of a world resisting control. Cold snaps and polar vortexes brutally compete against mass casualty heat waves, now a casual fact of life, like category six hurricanes.

She asks if it were really true about the sand and smiles skeptically as he replies, 'Before the jump yes, there were beaches like this everywhere.'

After the greater ice sheets break off the West Antarctic in the late twenty-first century, the world scrambles. A classic theological problem: what kind of gods foresee sin yet refuse to act? Something about free will. No, not satisfying. The first jump raises sea levels a good two metres in fifteen years.

'Even on the coasts there was sand?', she asks. Not accusatory, her tone. She doesn't know who to indict.

Every port and coastal city in the world is lost. The tide pushes sand up into abandoned streets of desolate cities, swamping estuaries and choking grass and trees in salt.

Food is already prohibitively expensive as crop yields on previously dependable farmland drop 50 per cent in a world struggling and failing miserably to support 10 billion mouths. Rations could be printed, but subscription fees keep the unemployed starving.

Capital trudges along, charting new ways to reap from the fires and wars even as economies drop 30 per cent in the West, 90 per cent in developing areas. The beginning of the permanent depression, the normal kind and the frightening.

'I wish you could have seen it', he replies.

The oligarchs close ranks, retreating to their bunkers and walled cities. Building new fiefdoms, amusement parks for their rotting souls. Sometimes the guards turn on the lords.

Communes spring up near fresh water, which is at least somewhat insulated from the melting. Some thrive. Most are suppressed by legal tricks of eminent domain or privatised police. The last undisturbed beaches in North America, along with the fresh water, draw waves of migrants north even as temperatures scorch the Midwest.

What else is there to say? Nearly everyone is displaced for reasons environmental or economic, to say nothing of war. Nobody but the luckiest live near family. The skies are milky white, never blue anymore, because of the stratospheric aerosols they released to dim the sun. Aside from the birds, most children haven't even seen a wild animal.

See, the Great Lakes are clustered aftermath of glacial retreat 10,000 years back. Glaciers covered much of North America at one point. When they melted away, they left rich soil deposits. Further back, shallow waters covered the American South during the Cretaceous period. Sea creatures died and their calcium carbonate exoskeletons accumulated. As carbon dioxide dropped and polar ice caps formed, the seas withdrew and left fertile soil. Millions of years later, that fertile soil of the Black Belt would draw slaveholders to plant cotton, tobacco, sugar, you name it. Set off a chain reaction of voracious capitalism and reactionary politics that, by the time climate change was discovered, stood poised and ready to murder every ecosystem locked up with resources, which was all of them. Very lucrative.

'Could there be beaches again, like on the ocean?', she asks innocently. Her grandfather weighs whether to wax poetic about the earth's ability to heal from ruin, the carbon drawdown cycles operating on timelines of thousands and millions of years. What a convoluted, cruel hope. They stole so much.

'No.'

LUÍSA CALVETE PORTELA BARBOSA

What's 'Left' of Lulism?

Bolsonaro's popularity is in apparent decline. Bolsonaro (currently, independent) projects the image of 'the outsider', despite having been in politics for decades. Most of these years were spent in the Progressive Party (PP) – the party with the highest number of politicians investigated for corruption. Three of his four sons are also in politics, and currently his whole family - ex-wife, included - are also being investigated. The charges include hiring fake employers with public money, including militia members (the 'rachadinha' scandal), spreading fake news, and attacks on democracy. Furthermore, Bolsonaro's government is being investigated in the ongoing Parliamentary Inquiry Commission (CPI) over his criminal dismissal of Covid-19 and the likely corruption behind the delayed purchase of overpriced vaccines. Brazil totals over 580,000 deaths from Covid-19 and thus, perhaps unsurprisingly, this inquiry became known as the 'CPI of death'. Attention to the investigation reached its peak in June-July 2021, when Brazilians were hooked to Parliament TV watching the CPI involve an ever-increasing number of government and military officials.

Making sense of Bolsonaro's government and actions is a

Homeric task. With every new scandal (and the closer his family members are to facing trial or being exposed), Bolsonaro issues a new sequence of fake and scandalous statements to divert attention. The most recent was the threat of a military coup during Brazil's Independence Day (7 September), which seems factitious given the presence of the military in all echelons of the government.

All eyes are now on the General Election of 2022. Currently, polls show an almost certain victory for Lula, who's been cleared to run for public office. But Bolsonaro has already responded by launching a campaign against the current voting system and threatening to suspend the elections. What seems puzzling is how Brazilians could move from Lula to Bolsonaro, and then back to Lula in such a short period of time.

The Left

Brazil has been a conservative part of the region since its formation when the Portuguese crown prince Dom Pedro declared the independence of the country in 1822 and became its Emperor. Brazil was the region's last country to entirely abolish its monarchy as well as slavery. As the region's largest economy, the conservative influence of its oligarchy-based political structure meant that the country was (and remains) a repressive force for the left in Latin America.

On the Latin American left, Marxism has long been the primary ideological influence. Yet vastly different interpretations of Marxism marked the institutionalisation of the left in Brazil. For example, the Brazilian Communist Party (PCB, founded in 1922) believed that the bourgeoisie would lead Brazil's path to communism. Therefore, the party adopted a strict 'stagist' view of development, hoping to copy the English experience described by Marx. For the PCB, Brazil struggled with feudalism and was still to enter its capitalist-industrial phase. Consequently, dissenting intellectuals, such as Caio Prado Jr., who believed Brazil was already capitalist ('a part of the great Portuguese enterprise') were excluded from the party.

Except for Mexico in 1910, where a revolutionary project was implemented, the region by and large pursued industrialisation as the solution to the problem of underdevelopment – the economic paradigm of the twentieth century. In Brazil, the 'national developmentalist' and authoritarian government of Getúlio Vargas (1930-45; 1951-54) imposed state-led industrialisation based on foreign investment, adding targeted social reforms. The rise of Developmentalism as a project helped to marginalise socialism, especially after the term was adopted by US foreign policy advisors.

Combining Cold War narratives with the excuse of development, US intervention was sold as a modernisation project. In reality, modernisation meant the privatisation of resources and suppression of peasant activism. The increasingly cosy relationship between US and Brazilian elites led to the 1964 civil-military coup when the country became another example of the US international 'military modernisation' campaign. Now in power, the Brazilian military became the champion of the US-formulated National Security Doctrine across the region, unifying the Southern American armed forces against the 'communist threat'.

When the coup took place, intellectual disagreements on the left had real consequences. The PCB saw the coup as a revolution; the industrial bourgeoisie had fulfilled its historical role of leading Brazil out of feudalism. Hence, the party failed to foresee the consequences of the coup and lead a unified opposition from the left. Among the dissident groups were the Marxist-Leninists of the National Liberation Action (ANL), who denounced the PCB's alliance with the bourgeoisie and with the removed president João Goulart. They also criticised the Party's belief in a non-violent revolution, even prior to 1964. Following the coup, Carlos Marighella became the leader of the ANL and of the armed struggle against the dictatorship. What followed is well-known: complete crackdown on social and political organisations, torture, killings, and disappearances. Marighella was killed in 1969 as 'Brazil's n.1 enemy', only a few months after the publication of his *Minimanual of the Urban Guerrilla* in the United States. Censorship hid both the violence as well as the failures of the regime, which amounted to increased indebtedness, poverty, inequality, and corruption. By the 1980s, the US had established its new paradigm of 'liberal democracy.' The military had to go, but not without the ruling elite securing its interests. This was the opposite of the 'development' that had been promised.

Among the many evils left behind by the regime is the creation of a coalition of opposition parties Brazilians call the 'centrão' ('big centre'). During the transition, this group rebuffed progressive policies in Parliament and built a veneer of neutrality around itself. They allegedly represent 'the middle-ground'. Thus, appeasing the centrão, the majority in Parliament, has remained central to any government since 1987. It is here that the story of the Partido dos Trabalhadores (PT) begins.

The PT Enters the Scene

The PT, founded in 1980, emerged from the congruence of trade unions, grassroots movements, and Base Ecclesial Communities at the end of the dictatorship (1964-85). With its roots in the trade union movement in São Paulo, the PT was a reformist party that proposed an alternative to both the Vargas model and communism. 'Democracy as universal value' was the consensus of the time, which the PT uncritically accepted. Meanwhile, leftist organisations criticised the bourgeois character of the proposed democracy, following the Leninist tradition. It is this 'neutral' discourse that the PT adopted as its official strategy in 1987, with the launch of its Popular Democratic Project (PDP).

The PDP continues to divide the Brazilian left. On the one hand, the PDP proposed concrete policies, such as defaulting on international debt and ending privatisations. On the other hand, it completely abandoned anti-capitalism and defended the 'accumulation of (political) forces', i.e. reform. By the time the 1988 Constitution came into force, the PT had amassed some success in local elections, and Lula had started to gain national prominence. Despite its small number of representatives in Congress, the Party also led the campaign against the Constitution, arguing for more social guarantees. This consolidated the PT as the voice of the 'left.'

But the victory of Fernando Collor de Mello in the first open election of 1989 cemented the PT's power-oriented strategy. Collor won with a slight margin against Lula, following a heavy anti-PT marketing campaign supported by the unholy alliance between political and business elites and the media. Throughout the 1990s, the PT continued to adapt its rhetoric. And by the time it finally came into power in 2002, most of the radical policies proposed in 1987 had been abandoned. Instead, big electoral donations and marketing campaigns came to the fore, leading to several changes in the party's strategic plans and branding. The PT even toned down the use of 'red' in its campaigns; a difficult task considering that its symbol is a red star. In this context, it is worth invoking Florestan Fernandes, who in 1991 asked, 'will the PT maintain its nature of the workers and social movements' historical needs if it prefers the "occupation of power" to the Marxist revolutionary optic?'

The PT in Power: Lula's liberal programme

The early 2000s were marked by economic crises across the region following the implementation of the Structural Adjustment Programmes. Brazilians faced a third term for the Brazilian Social Democracy Party (PSDB), which was facing a series of corruption allegations known as the 'privataria tucana.' The scandal exposed the enrichment of the high ranks of the party and the government during the privatisation of state companies, such as the mining giant Vale do Rio Doce and the national telecom company Telebrás. Unsurprisingly, voters opted for a more substantial change, increasing the participation of the left in Congress as well as resulting in the election of Lula. Moreover, the PT had successfully rebranded itself and managed to appease a section of the *centrão* during the election.

During the electoral campaign of 2002, Lula launched the 'Letter to the Brazilian People' directed at the transnational capitalist elite.

In the Letter, Lula promises to maintain the orthodox economic policies of Fernando Henrique Cardoso (alias FHC; 1995-2002). Still, when the polls leading up to the 2002 election showed a likely victory for Lula, Wall Street firms raised Brazil's risk rating. Brazil's currency lost value, and foreign investors pulled out of the country. All these trends continued following Lula's election and first day in office; of course, the Brazilian media was quick to point this out, continuing its campaign of discrediting the left.

Brazilian politics has always been dominated by the right. And conservative, liberal, and nationalist governments never fundamentally challenged the liberal economic basis of the country's elites. This means that leftist politics and agendas are historically misrepresented or completely side-lined by the mainstream media, pundits, and politicians. In this context, I would argue that it was not Lula's alleged leftism that appealed to voters but the belief in his exceptionalism.

Yet, once in power, Lula fulfilled the promise he had made to the elites in his 2002 letter. The PT government kicked off with the Zero Hunger campaign, which aimed to tackle inequality whilst signalling to the elite that the party could be trusted; after all, neither left nor right could claim ownership of 'ending hunger.' The story of the PT reveals the contradictions and limits of a conciliatory government. As Barbosa dos Santos writes, the 'Lulist model of regulating social conflict' rendered the PT effectively useless. But what is this model?

In his first year in power, Lula led the Workers' Party proposal of the pension scheme's reform, which furthered the liberal policies proposed by his predecessor. For example, the reform moved the management of part of the pensions to investment funds, corroding the logic of a collective, generational pension in favour of individual accumulation. It is worth noting that the PT had opposed some of the 2003 reforms when FHC was in government. But Lula's popularity and 'man of the people' image helped generate the kind of support for a liberal policy that FHC could only have dreamed of. The PT parliamentarians who continued to oppose the policies were expelled from the Party. This eventually led to the formation of the Socialism and Freedom Party (PSOL).

The PT thus presented itself as the party of a successful neo-developmentalism whilst adopting a clearly neoliberal agenda. Domestically, Brazil bet on the expansion of consumption and on credit for competitive companies to drive growth. In the backdrop of its so-called 'entrepreneurial diplomacy', exporters of primary products and construction companies received billions in incentive. As a result, Brazil's food industry boomed, and the country became the biggest exporter of meat in the world. The construction sector gathered even more attention: first, for its successful internationalisation; later, for mounting corruption cases. The relatively successful neoliberal reforms had brought with them a string of corruption cases that would haunt the PT for years to come. The first of these focused on the popular national oil company, Petrobras, and involved both construction companies and Lula.

But perhaps more important than corruption were the failures of the PT model. The industrial sector remained in the hands of multinational companies, and so did its revenue. Consequently, the PT turned to traditional sectors of the economy. The redirection toward large agribusiness and mining companies not only fed a sector that had historically opposed the Party (and the left), but also facilitated environmental and social catastrophes, such as Belo Monte and Mariana. The construction of Belo Monte in Amazonia united the PT with opposition parties against environmental experts, Indigenous leaders, and thousands of families that denounced the social and environmental impact of the dam. The controversy around private and public partnership reached a peak in 2015, when the municipality of Mariana was flooded with a toxic by-product of the nearby iron ore mine. Nineteen people were killed in the flood. The mud also reached the river Doce that feeds circa 230 cities, and the sea in the state of Espírito Santo; no detailed study of the effects of the disaster has been carried out.

The social impacts of the Party's liberal reforms are also apparent in the higher education sector where reforms parallel international trends. The PT was rightfully applauded for its extension of public university quotas in 2008 and 2012. After years of Black activism, public universities must now allocate 50 per cent of their vacancies to students with high school degrees from public schools and whose families earn one to one-and-a-half minimum wage salaries. A percentage of these quotas is redirected to students who self-identify as Black, Indigenous, and mixed race, according to the demographics of each state. This reform guarantees that students with similar backgrounds compete against each other in the universities' entrance exams (*vestibular*) and therefore have a higher chance of getting a better and totally free education.

Brazilian elites have misrepresented and opposed the reform from its inception. Yet, the PT overlooked the appeal and strength of this alliance between the media and the conservative and liberal elites. Instead, the party maintained its neoliberal agenda and coalition with the right. Notably, the real focus of the government's budget was the private sector which boomed during the PT's administration. The government subsidised private universities by offering flexible credit for students (i.e. ProUni, and Fies), targeting the lower classes. Consequently, 90 per cent of the new vacancies created during the PT's term were in fee-based, private universities. And while the sector grew exponentially, recent graduates found themselves highly indebted and thrown into a precarious and elitist job market that looks down on their qualification (public universities are considered elite institutions).

The PT government did enable some important advancements: absolute poverty was reduced and domestic work is better regulated, guaranteeing jobs and personal security for a large portion of the population. Workers' wages also increased and so did consumption and access to education. But the belief that the PT's popular support was unshakeable made the Party particularly vulnerable to attacks from the right. This became clear when power shifted back to the conservative elite in 2016. The events that followed also showed how the PT's reforms were not enough.

'The people on the street'

The widespread frustration and the political re-awakening of the capitalist establishment became apparent in 2013, when the announcement of a rise in transport tariffs led to a series of protests across the country later rebranded as 'anti-government' by the media. The PT was largely suspicious of the protesters, implying they were angry middle-class or poor people expecting too much. Yet for anyone who followed the protests on the ground, it was clear that these explanations were limited, if not ill-intentioned.

The first series of protests took place in the city of Natal, in August 2012. As more cities announced their budgets, the protests multiplied, reaching an apex in June 2013. Because the initial organisers of these actions were groups to the left of the PT, the media coverage followed its traditional line: across the country, news channels highlighted how the protests were disrupting traffic and the economy and focused on their supposedly violent nature. The protesters' reaction was to gather outside media conglomerate buildings where, unsurprisingly, the police were waiting to heavy-handedly disperse the crowd. The more violence, the more people joined. Solidarity protests continued even in cities where the tariff rise was revoked, calling not only for an end to the tariffs but for social reforms.

Then Mayor of São Paulo and presidential candidate in 2018, Fernando Haddad (PT) criticised the protests and defended the action of the military police – a legacy of the military dictatorship. Revealingly, so did the conservative governor of the state, Geraldo Alckmin (PSDB). By the end of June, it was estimated that 1.5 million people were on the streets. Hundreds of protesters had been arrested and attacked by the police, and one journalist had lost his eye after being hit by a rubber bullet. The media changed its tone in this context: the protests were now anti-Dilma, anti-PT, and anti-corruption. More and more people started to question if continuing the actions was a wise decision. After all, when the left is not the political norm, how to criticise it without facilitating the rise of the right?

Dilma was forced to address the nation and promised urban

and transport reforms. But the PT maintained what Arantes has called an urban 'anti-reform'. It was within the neoliberal paradigm that the PT oversaw the country's preparation for the World Cup of 2014 that was largely criticised by the population. How could a country riddled with inequality spend billions in football stadiums and high-end accommodation? Who would live there? Who could afford to attend the games?

By 2015, the economy was in a downward spiral, and between March and April another wave of national protests took off. Unlike in 2013, the 2015 protests were organised and financed by different liberal organisations with links to think tanks based in the US. Furthermore, the participants were mainly middle-class and upper-class white Brazilians in their 30s-50s. And the press exhibited evident support: televised news overlapped a biased coverage of corruption allegations with the coverage of the 'people on the street.' But despite the different contexts in which they emerged, both protests showed an inflexion of PT's political base: the Party could no longer claim ownership of the streets.

As corruption allegations mounted and the centrão changed sides, the impeachment of Dilma was decided. A technical and controversial pretext was found, and the impeachment vote happened in 2016. Watching the vote was sickening and telling of what was to come. Before announcing his vote, Bolsonaro's speech saluted the dictatorship and called Colonel Brilhante Ustra a hero, a particularly harrowing choice as Brilhante Ustra is known to have participated in torture sessions inflicted on Dilma. Worryingly, other members of the Congress similarly expressed a nostalgic conservatism in their voting speeches. Several parliamentarians made nods of support for the military, who they argued would bring order to an increasingly corrupt political system. Ironically, most of them are embroiled in corruption investigations themselves. Furthermore, echoing the pre-1964 coup demonstration in support of a military intervention – the March of the Family with God for Liberty – parliamentarians voted for the impeachment in 'defence of the Brazilian family', and 'of God' who, according to them, hates communism, corruption, and the PT.

With the impeachment, power went back to the hands of the conservative right-wing elite, and the 'communist threat' paradigm re-emerged. Since then, Brazil has been experiencing a new wave of politically motivated corruption investigations and prosecutions, as well as killings and disappearances. The most famous cases are the arrest of Lula in 2018, and the killing of Marielle Franco in March of the same year. Yet these cases need to be analysed alongside the rising number of crimes against Indigenous communities, the arrest of nine leaders of the squatting movement in São Paulo, the record high number of police killings, etc and etc. Together, these cases show how emboldened and violent the liberal-conservative establishment really is.

At the height of the 2018 election, Bolsonaro was campaigning from a hospital bed after a conspiracy-ridden knife attack, whilst Lula was in prison. Attempts by the PT to call Lula's arrest political were also clearly failing, and the Party was forced to field a new candidate. Lula convinced Fernando Haddad to replace him, but the campaign was centred on Lula. Not even the choice of a leftist deputy, Manuela D'Ávila (Communist Party of Brazil, PCdoB; formed in 1962), changed the PT's campaign strategy. Establishment candidates with national presence, such as Geraldo Alckmin (PSDB), and Henrique Meirelles (Brazilian Democratic Movement, MDB) received a neglectable percentage of votes. The right now faced an easy choice between the Party they had persecuted and Bolsonaro, who had voiced unwavering support for a liberal economy. They once again chose authoritarianism for the sake of 'freedom': economic but also political, as many now call the PT a communist party.

The PT seemed to believe the tiresome fallacy that the provision of social goods guarantees electoral success. But the rich ethnographic work of Brazilian scholars has shown that continuous marginalisation along with urban violence fed the politics of 'fear' and 'hate' responsible for the popularisation of the right. For example, Kalil et al (2021) have discussed the mobilising power of the fear of an international communist takeover. And Pinheiro-Machado and Scalco (2020) have looked at how the fear of an economic downturn fed into a violently masculine (or hateful) response towards progressive politics. Moreover, the work of these scholars shows how these discourses are not fixed. In fact, not even tropes we now associate with 'Bolsonarism' are attached to Bolsonaro. Discourses change, things happen, and different groups are de/re-mobilised.

What is perhaps more worrying about this realisation is that different threads associated with Bolsonaro are reaching people outside his electorate and are, in fact, international. For example, researchers and activists have warned of the spread of anti-vaccination fake news targeting Indigenous communities – a group with a historically high adherence to vaccination and overall rejection of Bolsonaro. Meanwhile, *centrão* candidates distance themselves from the government by openly criticising Bolsonaro but maintaining their alliance in Congress where 130 impeachment requests are waiting to be analysed. It is worrying how these liberal, conservative, and authoritarian voices are leading both the mainstream and the fringe, the 'common sense' and the 'revolt against the system.' In this seemingly apocalyptic scenario for the left, it is important to highlight the names that continue to work against this trend.

The Left beyond Lula

Bolsonaro's presidency has no silver lining, but it did facilitate an alliance between left-leaning parties. The next test will be the General Election of 2022. Two prominent names of the left are likely to run and win the governor's election in their home states, should the PT refrain from fielding candidates. With the participation of the PT, however, the left will be split, and a victory of right-wing candidates is certain.

Guilherme Boulos (PSOL) from São Paulo is undoubtedly on

the rise after decades of activism and political work. Boulos is one of the coordinators of the Homeless Workers' Movement (MTST) and has built solid support in his home state, currently larger than that of Haddad (PT). Boulos ascended nationally after joining the Presidential race in 2018, fairing very well in the debates. In 2020, Boulos ran for Mayor of São Paulo, and despite a small budget and only seventeen seconds on national TV for campaigning, he received 20 per cent of the votes, far more than any polls had predicted. Today, polls foresee a victory against the right-wing candidate Paulo Skaf (MDB), with a 10 per cent difference between the two.

Another important left candidate is Marcelo Freixo (Brazilian Socialist Party, PSB) from Rio de Janeiro. Freixo gained national prominence after he presided over the 'CPI of the militias' (2008) that investigated the relationship between politicians, businessmen and the police in the state of Rio de Janeiro. The CPI uncovered a complex web of favours, campaign funding, and violence that ultimately guaranteed the militias' control over deprived communities. Hundreds of policemen were arrested, and seven politicians were investigated – which has made Freixo a target ever since. A close friend of Marielle Franco, Freixo is a leftist figure in Brazil who has loudly denounced the Bolsonaro family and led the movement for a united anti-fascist front in the previous election. Currently, polls show his victory over Cláudio Castro (Liberal Party, PL) with a small margin. There is also a chance he will join forces with Lula, acting as his deputy.

Current governor of Maranhão, Flávio Dino, is another critical leftist leader who, along with Freixo, recently left the PCdoB to join the PSB. Dino has a high approval rating in his state. Openly communist and current president of the Legal Amazon consortium, he has been under continuous attack by right-wing groups. Randolfe Rodrigues (Sustainability Network, REDE) is the strong leader of the opposition in the Senate and a historical proponent of more radical economic policies. As such, Rodrigues is another leftist candidate to look out for.

These leaders have continued to rise despite the ascendance of the right. While they might give us hope, they also need our support. For a long time, the PT justified its distance from the left by arguing that an association would undermine the Party's chance of winning elections. But the PT's policy of compromise backfired: the centrão impeached Dilma, and the party now needs left allies to win any future elections. The PT also needs to retreat and build up its grassroots movements to help renew the narrative about the Party and the left in general. The story of the PT is a lesson that compromise is likely to lead to electoral defeat and the further encroachment of conservative politics. As Barbosa dos Santos summarised, non-oppositional approaches render leftist parties effectively useless.

To change this dynamic, parties (and any organisation) cannot refrain from challenging establishment discourse and policies. In the end, the most crucial question for Brazil is not where the left is, or who can replace Lula, but what kind of society is 'left' when the opposition retreats?

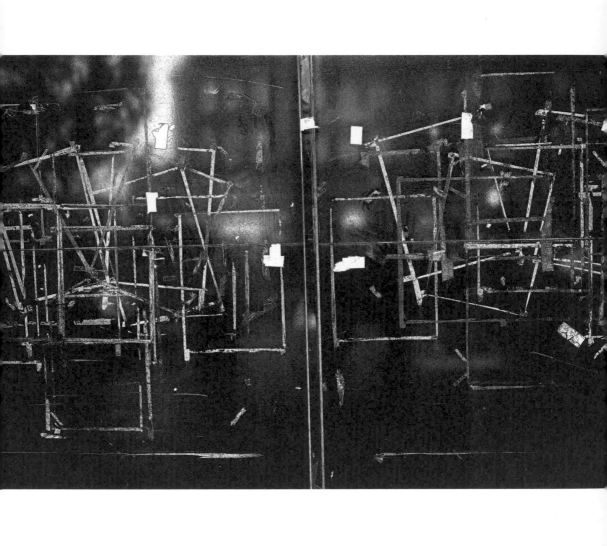

RICHARD SEYMOUR

That Beauty Which Hath Terror In It: In Praise of Nature Writing

To me the sea is a continual miracle,
The fishes that swim – the rocks – the motion of the
waves – the ships with men in them,
What stranger miracles are there?
– Walt Whitman, Miracles

Every creature points to God, none reveals Him.
– André Gide, The Fruits of the Earth

I.

Failing to reach the peak of Mount Ktaadn, lost in the fog, soaked through and sun-dried, almost out of food, finally descending in defeat through the Burnt Lands, arrested in the flow of description, gazing out at 'pure Nature ... vast and drear and inhuman', Henry David Thoreau is seized by rapture.

'I stand in awe of my body,' he exclaims in *The Maine Woods*,

this matter to which I am bound has become so strange
to me. I fear not spirits, ghosts, of which I am one – that
my body might – but I fear bodies, I tremble to meet
them. What is this Titan that has possession of me?
Talk of mysteries! Think of our life in nature, daily to
be shown matter, to come in contact with it, rocks,
trees, wind on our cheeks! the solid earth! the actual
world! the common sense! Contact! Contact! Who are
we? where are we?

Somehow that flayed encounter with the raw matter of being,
and the 'higher law' to which it pointed in the multiracial creed
of Transcendentalism, a non-parochial universalism, in which
every atom of every being was touched with divinity, was political.
As Laura Dassow Walls explains in her biography of Thoreau,
'this insight proved absolutely transformative'. Slavery was 'an
abomination to be stopped at any cost'. The subjugation of women
'must end'. Children 'must never be punished as sinners nor trained
as workers'.

Three years after his failed expedition, Thoreau published *On
Civil Disobedience*. Eight years later, in 1854, he wrote in a thundering
rage upon learning that the escaped slave Anthony Burns had been
returned to the slavers by the Boston authorities, and militant
abolitionists arrested following an attempted liberation: 'My
thoughts are murder to the State, and involuntarily go plotting
against her.' In 1859, he delivered his *Plea for Captain John Brown*,
in defiance of the overwhelming preponderance of white opinion:
the 'government menials', he was particularly pleased to note
when reflecting on Brown's violent delivery of human beings from
bondage, 'were afraid of him'. In nature, Thoreau had found not an
escape from entanglement with the social world, not an alternative
to political radicalism, but the 'confirmation of our hopes'.

One space spreads through all creatures equally –
inner-world-space. Birds quietly flying go
flying through us.
– Rainer Maria Rilke

II.

Thoreau's record of his 1846 trek through Maine's orogenous zones blazes with ambulatory excitement, even madness. The call of the wild, the days of hiking through dense forests of cedar, spruce and pine with vanishing trails, the perilous batteauing against the stream through vast rocky rivers, the minatory glide into dim lakes that swiftly conceal their exits to inexperienced travellers, the wading and climbing through further torrents toward a summit 'like a short highway, where a demigod might be let down to take a turn or two in the afternoon'... only for the whole enterprise to fail, gloriously fail, and give way to a transcendent geophany, a world-revelation.

The strangeness of matter. The estrangement of the body. Such experiences are surprisingly common. Barbara Ehrenreich describes an encounter with a wild, living cosmos, which sounds like a Transcendentalist delirium. 'The world flamed into life,' she writes in *Living With a Wild God*. 'There were no visions, no prophetic voices or visits by totemic animals, just this blazing everywhere. Something poured into me and I poured out into it.' The universe, a Heraclitean blaze. 'Each particle,' as Ralph Waldo Emerson wrote, 'a microcosm' of God.

The body which, as Walt Whitman said, 'balks account'. The sudden porosity of its boundaries: fiery atoms quietly flying through us. Here, thousands of miles from Selborne, is an 'original relationship to the universe' of the kind that Emerson sought. Not in Arcadia, but on the threshold of something terrible.

wild forest nature paths
heralding Resurrection
over and over again
– Margaret Walker, *Mississippi Spring*

III.

Amid the sad passions of the Anthropocene, with its corresponding deflation of desire, no one wants to be caught out in a naïve
enthusiasm. We are sensibly wary of such 'Thoreauvian pilgrimage',
as Lawrence Buell calls it. We are inoculated against what Kathryn
Schultz calls Thoreau's 'cabin porn': where the word 'porn' conveys
both knowingness and disapproval. We are scornful of the 'Lone
Enraptured Male' seeking 'wild places', as Kathleen Jamie cuttingly
quipped about Robert Macfarlane. We are embarrassed by rapture.
We know that there is no 'pure Nature', untouched. We find the rhetorical techniques of nature writing, what Timothy Morton calls
'ecomimesis', frequently clichéd and obvious.

We suspect that the hero's journey into the wild is saturated
with misanthropy and macho individualism, that it reeks of andro-
centrism and coloniality, that the wilderness aesthetic is loaded
with the ideology of the frontier, that the romance of sublime, wide-
open spaces is class-and-race gerrymandered (so pregnant with
massacres and enclosures), that the sense of 'discovery' in such
journeys manifests culturally-loaded ignorance, that making 'nature' the repository of the longing for transcendence is reactionary
and nostalgic, that the spiritual replenishment sought in the non-
human world is narcissistic and politically evasive, that the pan-
theistic vertigo of the spiritual traveller reduces to psychobabble,
that nature writing is in some constitutive manner 'white', and that
'nature' itself has been captured, commodified and converted into
a 'white' recreational pursuit.

Few are more attuned to the reactionary potential of nature
writing than nature writers. The bird-watcher and novelist Richard Smyth warns of the genre's 'fascist roots', from the Nazi Henry
Williamson, author of *Tarka the Otter*, to Edward Abbey's contempt
for the 'culturally-morally-genetically impoverished' immigrants
contaminating the North American landscape. Some of the most
passionate laments for nature, and defences of wilderness, have
come from the Right. Völkisch nationalism produced Ernst Moritz
Arndt's defence of the 'rights of wilderness' and the 'single unity' of
all nature, more than a century before Bolivia's Pachamama laws,

as well as Ludwig Klages' spitting contempt for the 'man of "progress"' announcing 'his masterful presence by spreading death and the horror of death' everywhere. Arndt's unitarian cosmos specifically excluded Jews, while Klages' indignation over the 'lawless and savage slaughter' by Europeans in North America was concerned, not about Indigenous people, but about the extermination of the buffalo. Even the mad dash for the mountain-top in search of wildness and the ecstatic dissolution of bodily boundaries may have a startling proximity to a version of fascist mysticism, as in Julius Evola's celebration of mountaineering as a self-conquering, spiritual quest.

We are accustomed to a critique of nature writing that, for intelligent reasons, assumes the perspective of a wary, disgusted, pedantic spectator. This is the libidinal ecology of historical defeat. The 'project of human history', Dominic Pettman writes, seems to be irreversibly suspended, or 'perhaps abandoned'. Given this, what is there to do but be on one's guard against seduction? 'Critique,' as Peter Wirzbicki laments in his history of black and white Transcendentalism, has 'replaced hope'. This is a bad place to get stuck.

> For a man-machine toil-tired
> May crave beauty too – though he's hired.
> – Claude McKay, *Joy in the Woods*

> Everything is mankind.
> – W E B Du Bois, *Darkwater*

IV.

As to the 'whiteness' of nature writing, it is an artefact – not of the absence of black nature writing, even of bad black nature writing – but of the exclusions of a genre, dixit Rebecca Solnit, 'barricaded with omissions to make it just another gated community'.

Not that the genre doesn't include Eddy L Harris' defiantly Thoreauvian solo pilgrimage down the Mississippi, Raja Shehadeh's anti-colonial poetics of 'sarha', a 'letting go' that gives one 'a drug-free high, Palestinian-style', Jini Reddy's attempt to re-enchant the earth beneath her feet, Zakiya McKenzie's forest poetry, Anita Sethi's anti-racist declaration of belonging in the Pennines, Langston Hughes' lament for lost trees and 'silver moons', Du Bois' spiritual descent into dark waters and 'the entrails of the earth', the stunning natural vistas in Richard Wright's landscape portrait of twelve million black American lives, Sudesh Mishra's hymn to Skye, Evelyn White's trembling hesitation about the outdoors, the historical and poetic works of Dorset author Louisa Adjoa Parker, Alice Walker's worshipful acknowledgment of flowers, landscape and the colour purple, Elizabeth-Jane Burnett's 'geological memoir' of Devon, Albery Allson Whitman's celebration of Seminole and Maroon resistance to the United States as a triumph of Nature over Mammon, and the nature poems of Ed Roberson, Camille T Dungy, Claude McKay, Rita Dove, and Jean Toomer. But the shelves of major bookshops, anthologies and nature writing prizes have only recently begun to notice.

The traditional exclusions of nature writing are a regional expression of a more general segregation built into how racial capitalism configures one's metabolic relationship to the natural environment, how one's class context situates one as 'rural' or 'urban', and how the caloric energy is extracted from one's body, rendering one either 'natural' or 'civilized'. It confers different sensibilities, different ambivalences. In *Black Nature*, Dungy observes that black nature writing 'only conforms ... in limited ways' with what has been known in 'the Western intellectual canon, spawned by the likes of Virgil and Theocritus and solidified by the Romantics and Transcendentalists'. Black authors 'simply do not look at their environment from the same perspective of Anglo-American writers'.

The point feels slightly overstated, and not just because of the absolute lack of homogeneity in the 'Western intellectual canon' being described here: there are gulfs of social experience and artistic style between the Virgilian pastoral, the Renaissance neo-pastoral, eighteenth-century labourers' poetry, and the Romantics and Transcendentalists. Black nature writing is as likely as its 'Anglo-American' counterpart to rhapsodise nostalgically, to mourn losses in nature, to find in it refuge, spiritual journey, ego-death and replenishment. The hallmark of the Romantic style, writes Raymond Williams in *The Country and the City*, is that the nature poet has become a 'lonely observer who "passes"', encountering nature as a 'still life'. 'People', he writes, begin to say, 'the city' when they mean 'capitalism or bureaucracy or centralised power.' 'Nature', or the 'country' stands for 'everything from independence to deprivation, and from the powers of an active imagination to a form of release from consciousness'. This social experience appeared earlier in England than elsewhere because of the precocious arrival of agrarian capitalism, and colonial plunder reducing the demand for domestic agricultural productivity. But it has generalised. And yet, there is in black nature writing a distinctive kind of ambivalence, the tonal imprint of the Du Boisian 'double consciousness'.

In *12 Million Black Voices*, Richard Wright's landscape portrait of black life in the United States, the natural environment taunts its rural subjects with what it has to offer. 'Our southern springs are filled with quiet noises and scenes of growth', Wright begins, establishing the familiar rhythm and lyric of nature writing. 'Apple buds laugh into blossom. Honeysuckles creep up the sides of houses. Sunflowers nod in the hot fields.' But then, almost as soon as this thought is verbalised, there comes another to undercut it. 'They,' he writes, 'have painted one picture: idyllic, romantic; but we live another; full of fear of the Lords of the Land, bowing and grinning when we meet white faces, toiling from sun to sun, living in unpainted wooden shacks that sit casually and insecurely upon the red clay'. 'Landscapes can be deceptive', John Berger writes, 'Sometimes a landscape seems to be less a setting for the life of its inhabitants than a curtain behind which their struggles, achievements and accidents takes place.' In English literature, as Raymond Williams put it, 'a working country is hardly ever a landscape.' But what other sort of landscape could there be for those who toil 'from sun to sun'?

After the great surges of urbanisation in the twentieth century, it is now 'as if', said the captions to Ingrid Pollard's 'Pastoral Interludes', 'the black experience is only lived within an urban environment'. The 'whitening' of nature, from Homesteading to 'white flight' and exurbanism, begets a bitter, violent separation, and a brutal aesthetic impoverishment for those who are excluded. Environmental injustice leaves nine million people exposed to hazardous waste sites across the United States, write Lauret Savoy and Alison Deming in *The Colors of Nature*, half of them 'people of colour'. 'You got trees all dappled with sunlight and shit,' G E Patterson writes in 'The Natural World':

> I got trees too   My trees stainless steel poles ...
> You got birds waking you up in the morning ...
> I got birds too ...
> My birds   My birds   killers.

Nature is further 'whitened' by the fear of rural racism, begetting a trembling ambivalence. Evelyn White describes a 'fear' of the natural environment, 'like a heartbeat, always present, while at the same time intangible, elusive and difficult to define'. The 'river's roar', she writes, 'gave me a certain comfort', but 'I didn't want to get closer. I was certain that if I ventured outside to admire a meadow or to feel the cool ripples in a stream, I'd be taunted, attacked, raped, maybe even murdered because of the colour of my skin'. Pollard describes 'a feeling of unease, dread', a 'feeling I don't belong.' Walks 'through the leafy glades' are undertaken 'with a baseball bat by my side'. Even Eddy L Harris begins his wilfully dangerous and wild journey down the Mississippi, in *Mississippi Solo*, with a friend cautioning him that he'll be travelling 'from where there ain't no black folks to where they still don't like us much. I might be a little concerned about that.' This is the dread that rustles under the surface when Lucille Clifton strives to write of the trees waving their knotted branches, but finds 'under that poem/always an other poem'.

The second sight of the doubly conscious, in the Du Boisian idiom, derives from racial injury and humiliation. Yet it is, not a disfigurement, but the motor of a transcendental striving: much as, perhaps, the double alienation of the working-class is what is supposed to constitute it as the 'universal class'. Decades before Du Bois used the term 'double consciousness' in *The Souls of Black*

Folk, it had been used by Emerson to describe the dilemma of a Transcendentalist continuously pulled between the 'buzz and din' of daily life, the social forces inhibiting self-development, and the 'infinitude and paradise' of transcendence. For Du Bois, the 'African' pole of the African-American psyche points to transcendence. According to Dickson Bruce, this opposition works as a deliberate figurative background in Du Bois' deployment of 'double consciousness'. In *Darkwater*, a memoir and spiritual prospectus for racial salvation, he seeks out infinitude and paradise in the natural world. He pleads for such a relationship to nature, not just as a refuge for those 'scarred in the world's battle and hurt by its hardness', but as essential to the 'utter joy of life'. There is the disgrace of the segregated railway car and the internal frontiers known as Jim Crow. There is also the 'sunset and moonlight on Montego Bay in far Jamaica'. And 'both things are true and both belong to this our world, and neither can be denied.' The duplicity, the doubleness of the world, begets double-vision.

In passages redolent of Thoreau and Whitman, Du Bois describes his travels 'over seven thousand mighty miles' across the United States, culminating in a visit to the Grand Canyon. 'It is awful,' he writes, in ecstatic mood:

> There can be nothing like it. It is the earth and sky gone stark and raving mad. The mountains up-twirled, disbodied and inverted, stand on their peaks and throw their bowels to the sky. Their earth is air; their ether blood-red rock engreened. You stand upon their roots and fall into their pinnacles, a mighty mile. ... One throws a rock into the abyss. It gives back no sound. It falls on silence – the voice of its thunders cannot reach so far. It is not – it cannot be a mere, inert, unfeeling, brute fact – its grandeur is too serene – its beauty too divine! It is not red, and blue, and green, but, ah! the shadows and the shades of all the world, glad colorings touched with a hesitant spiritual delicacy. What does it mean – what does it mean? Tell me, black and boiling

water! It is not real. It is but shadows. The shading of
eternity.

That familiar sequence of events. A pilgrimage to somewhere
manifestly made by a force vastly greater and older than humanity:
deep time. Eternity, as Lauret Savoy writes of the same landscape
almost a century later in *Trace*, suggested by 'one frame of an
endless geologic film'. Familiar outlines of world, self, up, down,
in, out, disintegrating. Dread becoming awe. The pilgrim goes mad
with questions.

Swimming and dreaming were becoming indistinguish-
able. I grew convinced that following water, flowing with
it, would be a way of getting under the skin of things, of
learning something new. I might learn about myself, too.
In water, all possibilities seemed infinitely extended.
– Roger Deakin, *Waterlog*

I've known rivers ancient as the world and older than
the flow of human blood in human veins. I bathed in the
Euphrates when dawns were young. I built my hut near
the Congo and it lulled me to sleep. I looked upon the Nile
and raised the pyramids above it. My soul has grown deep
like the rivers.
– Langston Hughes, *The Negro Speaks of Rivers*

V.

Nature writing, as 'ecomimesis', tries to convince us that we are in
the thick of it. It strives to cultivate a planetary sensibility of being
in the flow, aerial, ambulatory or natatory, the body merging and
moving with its environment. We are to 'take part in its existence', as
Keats partook of the life of a sparrow outside his window. The logic,
as Timothy Morton acknowledges in his critique of nature writing,
is that 'if we could not merely figure out but actually experience the
fact that we were embedded in our world, then we would be less
likely to destroy it.'

Much depends on the kind of nature we ambiently experience.

Nature is ordinary but, as Kate Soper has remarked, the 'nature' of poetic writing is generally not 'the kind of thing we eat for breakfast'. The salmon that Thoreau and his comrades fried for breakfast next to Lake Ambejejus was not the nature that inspired him to rapture, any more than Kenneth Clark was inspired by the form of culture that appeared in *The Racing Post*. Both 'Nature' and 'Culture', in this sense, are for spectators. We visit, and contemplate, but do not participate. Yet this suggests that any nature worth writing about is always somewhere else.

Must nature writing, to achieve its world-defamiliarizing, transcendent effect, take us to Great Scenery – forests, islands, frozen seas, mountains, ocean floors, jungle canopies, river deltas, landscapes criss-crossed with hedgework forming rumpled parallelograms – made remote by the territorial matrix of the capitalist state? How can a planetary sensibility, if it is to inform practical life rather than providing a reliably commodified unplugging from it, survive on nothing more than second-hand awe? Worse than ineffectual, Morton suggests, such remote admiration for a capitalised 'Nature' 'does for the environment what patriarchy does' for women. As 'a paradoxical act of sadistic admiration', it is a catalyst of the Anthropocene. In other ways, the category of 'Nature' is implicated in a moral hierarchy of being, girding the violent codification of bodies as either natural (Stefanie Dunning notes the 'stunning parallelism' in the 'treatment of both the natural world and Black people') or unnatural (the Nazi idea of 'Jewish unnatur' has been taken up by ecofascists) and therefore as fungible, exploitable, disposable and murderable.

Nature writing has traditionally been sustained by what Jason W Moore calls the great 'Cartesian Divide' between nature and humans. Humans can 'visit' nature only if we are not of it. The 'new nature writing', however, has set out to unravel this conceptual artifice. Studies of the 'wild' are now palimpsests of historical, geological, philosophical, political and literary commentary, alongside natural observation. 'Nature is not now, nor has ever been, a pure category,' Robert Macfarlane writes in *Landmarks*. 'We inhabit a post-pastoral terrain'. 'The needs of the natural world,' Richard

Mabey writes in *The Unofficial Countryside*, 'are more prosaic' than the poetics of sublimity would suggest. 'A crack in the pavement is all a plant needs to put down roots.' There are almost as many trees in London, Paul Wood reminds us, as there are people. The ecologist Anders Pape Møller finds vastly more birds living in small towns, alongside humans, than in the countryside. Hence, perhaps, the growing popularity of urban and liminal spaces, in Paul Farley and Michael Symmons Roberts' chronicle of the *Edgelands*, Iain Sinclair's psychogeographies of the urban margins, and Cal Flynn's exploration of disaster zones abandoned by human beings, and flourishing.

On the other side of the great divide, is culture. We have been given to believe that 'culture' belongs to humans while 'nature' belongs to everything else. It is not so. Animals of many kinds exhibit culture, symbolic life and even, in some cases, rudimentary forms of language. 'All chimpanzees climb trees,' Carl Safina writes in *Becoming Wild*, 'that's not cultural. Some chimpanzees crack nuts with hammer stones and anvils, but not every population that lives where there are nuts cracks them. It's cultural.' Sperm whales and elephants survive thanks to the accumulated environmental knowledge of elders: that is cultural. Chimpanzees have fashion trends, according to Primatologists from the Max Planck Institute for Psycholinguistics in Nijmegen: that, too, is cultural. Orca communities self-segregate for reasons that are entirely cultural. 'Chaser the border collie has learned the names of more than a thousand toys and understands grammar,' Eva Meijer writes in *Animal Languages*. 'Dolphins living in the wild call one another by name. Prairie dogs have an extensive language for describing intruders … Elephants in captivity can speak in human words … The languages of whales, octopuses, bees and many birds have a grammar.' All of which is culture. Or, to steal a Harawayan term of art, natureculture.

Is there anything left of 'nature'? Must the category of nature keep 'giving writers the slip', as Morton suggests? Yes, and no. There can be no 'after nature', simply because, after all interminglings and hybridisms between the natural and social are accounted for, nature still exists, and is still distinct from the social. Historical materialists are substance monists: we do not think there is any kind of substance other than matter. Andreas Malm, however, insists that we must be 'property pluralists'. There are hierarchies of matter: the matter of quarks and atoms, the matter of chemistry, of molecules and compounds, the cellular matter of biological life, and the material practices and rituals of social life. Each layer of matter has its own emergent qualities. For example, it is only when carbon and oxygen atoms combine to form a carbon dioxide molecule that they are capable of preventing infrared radiation from escaping the planet's atmosphere, thus warming it up: the process known as 'radiative forcing'. The social, similarly, is an emergent property of the natural. Carbon dioxide in the atmosphere will always warm the planet, but only a human society organised by capitalist industry is capable of ripping fossil sunlight out of the earth's lithosphere and converting it into heat energy with carbon dioxide as an industrial byproduct in sufficient quantities to cause catastrophic global heating. The layers of matter are mixed in various ways, but they are still distinct because of their unique properties. As a special case of this 'property pluralism', where environmental destruction is concerned, Malm argues that we must be property dualists. It is at the interface between society and nature, and not that 'between droplet and cloud', or between carbon atom and carbon dioxide molecule, that the cataclysm is taking place: once again, duality in the world begets doubleness of consciousness. And it is that interface, among other things, that a planetary sensibility seeks to revolutionise.

> We must and will get used to the chill, yea, to the cosmic chill, if need be.
> – John Burroughs, *Time and Change*

VI.

Script is on the side of annihilation. Writing is a special form of dead labour which prolongs the life of perception, memory, experience, calculation and desire. It is, in the vocabulary of evolutionary biologists, 'cumulative culture', a force-multiplier. Civilization, from the dynastic states of Egypt and Mesopotamia, to the digitally written systems of late capitalism, is unimaginable without this social learning. *Homo sapiens* is an evolutionary ingenue. We have nothing on what Heathcote Williams described as the 'fifty-million-year-old sagas of continuous whale mind'. *Homo scribens*, however, is the apex predator on the planet. The abstractive properties of writing allow the matter of the world to be transformed into 'a carefully patrolled domain of phantom entities', as David Wengrow puts it.

Homo scribens is already complicit in the Anthropocene, the geological epoch of humanity in its capitalist phase. All social orders are written, from contract to constitution. The metabolic flow of a society depends on its being remembered and automated. No society, however, is as constituted by the violence of written abstractions as one dominated by the capitalist mode of production. The unprecedented accumulation of script under capitalism is harnessed to its accelerating metabolisation of fungible labour and fungible nature. The thaumaturgy of writing transforms surplus labour and cheap nature into tradeable titles to surplus value, a dance of phantom entities.

Popular nature writing, though morally armed against what Donald Worster calls the 'Imperial' tradition which inscribes nature with value for the purposes of extraction and domination, is often complicit in this. At its worst, as Joe Kennedy scoffs in *The Authentocrats*, it purveys a mass-produced, commodified 'idea of wildness' while quietly campaigning 'for a patriotic traditionalism'. It is, moreover, unconsciously loaded with violent abstractions in which the energetic flux of matter has already been appropriated and codified as a property relation. To merely describe a 'forest', as Robert Macfarlane acknowledges in *Landmarks*, is to refer to the medieval act of enclosure through which woodlands were reserved as hunting grounds for royalty. A hedgerow is often a residue of the primitive accumulation of capital, ancient class violence, and property claims. Even where they have not been planted for enclosure, Oliver Rackham's *The History of the Countryside* suggests, they have often grown around the fences ringing property thanks to birds 'sitting and dropping seeds'.

In the tradition of nature writing, a decorous veil is frequently drawn over this social warfare. 'Sidney's *Arcadia*,' Raymond Williams reminds us, 'was written in a park which had been made by enclosing a whole village and evicting the tenants.' Robert Herrick's *The Hock-Cart or Harvest Home* enjoins the labouring tenants of the Earl of Westmoreland's estate: 'And, you must know, your Lord's word's true,/Feed him ye must, whose food fills you.' The 'labouring poets' of the eighteenth century were Royal-approved bards of duty, deference and diligence. Stephen Duck, in *The Thresher's Labour*, supplies polite society with a fatalistic ideological defence of the class system: 'Let Poverty, or Want, be what it will,/It does proceed from God, therefore's no ill'. At worst, the ecocentric disposition does not so much veil as make the case for such violence. Consider Dave Foreman, one of the founders of Earth First. 'I am an animal,' he writes in *Confessions of an Eco-Warrior*.

> The oceans of the Earth course through my veins, the winds of the sky fill my lungs, the very bedrock of the planet makes my bones. I am alive! ... When a chain saw slices into the heartwood of a two-thousand-year-old Coast Redwood, it's slicing into my guts. When a bulldozer rips through the Amazon rain forest, it's ripping into my side.

And when famine tears through Ethiopia? 'The best thing would be,' he told an interviewer, 'to just let nature seek its own balance, to let the people just starve there.'

And yet, there is also this: Thoreau *losing his mind* in the mountains of Maine, Du Bois descending into the entrails, rapturous, each finding in this a value for life other than the value-form, adding it to our social intelligence. There are, in other words, the resistant properties of writing. The linguistic anthropologist Piers Kelly has described the emergence of several writing systems precisely through the efforts of populations resisting their oppression or extinction. Nature writing, styling matter, moulding experience at the interface, inflaming readers with biophilic joy, can undo some of the epistemological violence of capital which renders nature 'cheap' and exploitable. It can be counter-extinction. If we disparage this effort in the name of a critical procedure that is always on guard against seduction, we will have succumbed to a form of spiritual defeatism.

> That beauty which, as Milton sings/Hath terror in it.
> – William Wordsworth, *The Prelude*

> The numberless goings on of life/inaudible as dreams.
> – Samuel Taylor Coleridge, *Frost at Midnight*

VII.

Birds are planetary. The Jurassic Coast is visited by puffins with homes in northern Scotland, skuas and terns flying south from the Arctic, kittiwakes returning from winter in the Atlantic, spoonbills from Mauritania and Senegal. There, in the summer months, life is composed of sea thrift, sea campion, sea kale, sea bindweed, bright red cinquefoil, red campion, mikoikoi, ribworth plantain, tree mallow, Spanish bluebell, hogweed, trailing bellflower, perennial cornflower, florist's cineraria, bristly oxtongue, artichoke thistle, hoary stock, scot's broom, gorse, beet, sow-thistle, lichen-gilded stones, Norway maples, limes, elderflowers, sycamores, earth slicks and quicksilver puddles, bowers, blooms, blossoms, branches, grass snakes, trickles of water gurgling under pileous hedges and shrubs, falling down plunging telluric crevasses into the sea, nettles, dock weed, goosegrass, the coiled counterforms of ammonites, petrified wood and pyrite trilobites: history on the scale of hundreds of millions, all thickly layered with vibrant detail like a Pollock painting.

Sap smells pungent in the sun. The dark drench-dried green weed sticks flat to the cool surface of chalky stone lathed and drilled by the tide and its sandy freight. From the shade, sunlight glimmers over the white ledge: a lime-light. The tide brings with it slick swarms of seaweed and macroalgae. The air smells of sea vapour, rich with the sex pheromones of seaweed, the aromatic chemicals produced by marine worms, and the fragrance of dead phytoplankton being devoured by bacteria. For this smell, there is the French word, 'embrun'. On the pebble beach, sun-died kelp release a rich, salty death odour. A gust of gulls takes off, like shell-coloured leaves. Courteous predators, civil parasites picking off discarded flesh, confident among humans. They chuckle, kee-awe, and emit longer melancholy sounding moans, like banshee wails in miniature.

In these parts, the cliffs, notoriously subject to land slippage, reveal strata of an ancient sea-bed, studded with remnants of extinct creatures, picked and sold on seafront shops: petty fossil-capital. A slip of the land is an unintentional revelation. On the Jurassic Coast, the earth shows us some of what it has been up to. From the perspective of 'deep time', the land is an uncovered sea-bed while the sea is a slow flood. In past eons, this was an ocean. Later, it was reptile kingdom, land-locked, tropical. Much as the peaks of the Alps once lay under the sea of Tethys between the ancient continents of Gondwana and Laurasia, the rocky surface which was once the floor of a teeming marine life is now host to snow leopards, wolves, marmots, and golden eagles.

The world under pandemic emergency measures felt terribly old. Its convulsions of flooding, wildfire, mass extinction, ocean acidification, arctic fire, ice sheet melt, and now a zoonotic plague, were those of a dying planet. Here, on the well-trodden south-west coastal path, the planet was still thriving. It was not utopian, but it was easy to feel that it was. I, cheerfully enraptured, enjoyed in echo, as a second-hand emotion repeating itself, a duplication of a duplication, something I had felt upon reading John Muir, 'discovering' Glacier Bay in southeast Alaska, bounding up the mountain sides while his Stickeen guides slept, breathlessly sketching everything under what Coleridge would have called 'the secret ministry of the moon'. And returning at dawn, ecstatic, his 'mind glowing like the sun-beaten glaciers', 'too happy to sleep'. The world seemed young to that explorer.

JULES JOANNE GLEESON

Histories of People, Histories of Rupture

History has an ambivalent character, and has proven an unreliable servant for any political cause. Since the twentieth century, innumerable researchers have been drawn towards the question of gay history – both what 'our' history looks like, and at what point 'we' became gays at all.

Let's focus here on history as a set of research practices, rather than professional institutions. Considering history as a field, it will suffice to say that world historic breakthroughs around 'acceptance' in the rest of society have not always ensured clear pathways for those hoping to entrench themselves in history faculties. Those hoping to cultivate lasting careers are generally expected to position 'LGBT history' as one concern alongside a broader range of research interests.

The result is that history shares with philosophy the status of a relatively respectable field within the humanities, especially in contrast to 'area studies' of any focus, or studies of the literary. But the reality is that its 'rigour' depends on a routinised downplaying of overt involvement in the stakes at hand. (Consider, for instance, the impact Gayle Salamon and Saidiya Hartman have had on the fields of philosophy and history respectively, without finding a natural place in those disciplines' respective faculties.)

But let's set aside history as an institutionally founded discipline, and focus instead on the double-edged character of historical practice as a way of thinking through political problems. This will cast some light on the unreliable character of history as a means of thinking through social change, and movements.

Let's begin by setting out two overarching hopes gays (etc.) have for history.*

1. **'A People With A History'**: a commonplace exercise where LGBT people trace sexuality as a people (apparently equivalent to an ethnicity), which existed with varying degrees of institutional recognition and popular acceptance across time.

2. **Gay Genealogies**: these approaches stress the *discontinuous* form taken by normative understandings of sex and sexuality, and as such the constantly shifting place of perceived 'deviation'.

The first approach treats gay or LGBT people as a population to be identified across time. (The term 'People With A History' I draw from the dedicated sub-site of the Fordham Sourcebook's *Online Guide to Lesbian, Gay, Bisexual and Trans* History*, run by John Halsall). An exemplary figure in this approach was the medievalist and Church historian John Boswell (known to his friends as 'Jeb'), who enjoyed unique popular acclaim among pre-modern historians of his day.

In *Christianity, Social Tolerance and Homosexuality* (1980), Boswell re-examined the historical record of the Roman Catholic

---

*As with any dichotomy this division is established for the purposes of illumination, and will duly collapse under closer inspection.

Church, arguing that it revealed an underappreciated legacy of tolerance. His follow up monograph, *The Marriage of Likeness: Same-Sex Unions in Pre-Modern Europe* (1994), expanded Boswell's study to include a pre-modern rite concerned with making unrelated men brothers (Adelphopoiesis). Boswell used the prevalence of this liturgical form to argue for a widely attested, ecclesiastically approved, and public validation of same-sex relationships.

But these claims attracted considerable controversy, and subsequent scholarship within specialist fields has largely contradicted Boswell's provocative thesis. (A noble, if perhaps still not exhaustive, attempt to catalogue the furore around Boswell's reading of Adelphopoiesis rites can be found in the Fordham Sourcebook's *Online Guide*). At the time, however, Boswell's work achieved a certain caché for two reasons: firstly, his standing as a Yale Professor and open affiliation with Catholicism made it difficult to dismiss him as either a fringe scholar or hostile voice. Secondly, the notion of 'same-sex unions' extending from pre-modernity presented not simply a picture of 'homosexual tendencies' and their repression as an ongoing site of social conflict; rather, it proposed a more settled and even normatively accepted framework for male-male relationships. Boswell's work could therefore be accurately classed as an investigation into the 'history of tolerance' as the history of homosexuality.

Boswell's historical claims were perfectly fitted to advancing what we might call the mainline liberal position for gay acceptance in the later twentieth century: that homosexuality was a minority of the population attested across historical eras; that institutional recognition had existed previously and could be fruitfully offered again; that homophobia was a political or ideological project that could never hope to suppress the trans-historical reality of homosexual impulses and companionship; and that hostile voices which asserted themselves as guardians of 'tradition' were in fact operating from a place of profound ignorance.

For decades this first ('ethnicising') approach to gay history has been criticised by both political and methodological radicals. They argue that these attempts to historicise gay life often amount to urbane wealthy homosexual guys turning their gaze across historical sources to find experiences that match their own. In the process, they efface particular positions that are less commensurate with today's 'scene life'.

As well as developing these critiques, literary historians including Carolyn Dinshaw (focusing on the medieval English canon) and Heather Love (in her work on the irresistible lure of miserable fiction) have brought into view not only historical communities, but the exercise of historical thinking that draws historians and other readers into contact with minorities they have no direct contact with. Dinshaw and Love stress trans-historical contact as something which has to be delicately attempted, rather than assumed: a people who become such *through* history, one might say.

Other historians have focused on gay history not as an exercise in uncovering a 'people' but a sensibility or aesthetic. (Robert Atkins' 1966 essay 'Goodbye Lesbian/Gay History, Hello Queer Sensibility: Meditating on Cultural Practice' presents a critical take on this shift). Gay history is also defended by Christopher Castiglia and Christopher Reed's book *If Memory Serves: Gay Men, AIDS, and the Promise of the Queer Past* (2011), in an approach best classified as 'history of memory'.

Despite decades of skilled critiques levelled against it, the 'ethnicising' approach has resisted being dispensed with. There are two simple reasons for this: firstly, the rarity of coming to queer consciousness in a familial household means that familiarising oneself with gay life across previous eras will remain a neccessity. Secondly, popular phobias ensure that the public sphere will often be cluttered with confidently expressed claims that bear no relation to the historical record. In this context, ripostes and correctives become simple enough.

I recall here a recent episode where a British philosophy professor opined on social media that no transgender woman would have had the nerve to refer to herself as a lesbian prior to a decade ago. It was simple enough to find a strip from *Dykes to Watch Out For* (signed by its artist Alison Bechdel 1995, bottom right): the twenty-six-year-old strip refutes any notion of '90s lesbian and trans culture being tidily separable, even as it attests to the longstanding resistance among some cis

lesbians towards that *de facto* merger. (Though its hopeful ending suggests this could be overcome through acts of solidarity). Shortly after her remarks, I did my best to bring this cartoon to the attention of the philosophy professor in question, but have not yet received a reply.

To prove that one has existed, and been recorded as being there, may be a remedial work from one view. Yet resisting these empty claims of novelty is work which often won't do itself.

This response through the 'power of pedantry' is both important and ensures easy wins: those who aren't members of a minority group have a weaker grasp of their history (for the most part). The most hateful might be prone to vague speculations based on popular stereotypes, and resulting embarrassment when their musings are compared to the harsh glare of the historical record. While social emancipation cannot be reduced to debaters' back-and-forths alone, these moments may afford the historically informed with a certain advantage of position.

There are clear limits to how many political victories can be won through disputes over points-of-fact. But this 'popular' face of queer history does not seem likely to exhaust itself yet. Resisting political projects which seek to entrench phobic sentiments or keep civil rights stripped will often require rebutting historical claims considerably more crude and oblivious than the fine details of terminological breakthroughs which historical constructionists tend to concern themselves with.

Genealogical investigation into homosexuality is typically associated with Michel Foucault, who drew on Friedrich Nietzsche's tendency to sort ideas by their pedigree. While an early admirer of Boswell's work, Foucault's account came to provide a new sketch of heterosexuality, which he presented as a novel normative order originating in the nineteenth century.

The prominent place of gay genealogical investigation (otherwise known as historicist or constructionist accounts of homo/heterosexual identity) was ushered into the twenty-first century through the work of classicist David Halperin, who between his books *One Hundred Years of Homosexuality* and *How To Do the History of Homosexuality* advanced an increasingly refined, yet strictly orthodox Foucauldian perspective. In this view, prior eras drawn on by modern readers as instances of an ancient gay history (particularly ancient Greece) in fact operated according to incommensurate conceptions of sexuality and, indeed, had little overt comprehension of 'sexuality' as a concern at all.

Genealogical approaches are often at odds with efforts to trace trans-historical communities or movements, instead stressing the place of frameworks and conceptions specific to historical eras – both as decisive features of social life and continuously manipulated instruments of powerful institutions. As Thomas Moynihan's *Spinal Catastrophism: A Secret History* (2019) has it, genealogy is a work of unveiling:

> [Genealogy] works to reveal that those beliefs that we think depend upon *edifying reasons* in fact depend upon *contingent causes*, unveiling unaccountabilities in the structure of belief. Thus one may be seen to hold a particular belief not on account of deliberative ratiocination, but as a result of some accident of background or upbringing.

In the gay context, geneaological historians not only stress contingency but also *discontinuity*: the ways in which figures who may appear easily recognisable at first glance upon closer inspection may be mutually incommensurate – far harder to comprehend than initial recognition may suggest.

For obvious reasons, this makes genealogy a tool as likely to be disruptive of appeals to gay history attempted for the sake of emancipatory politics as accounts which stress the novelty of LGBT life. This is a necessary sacrifice. Much of the analytic power of this approach comes exactly from setting aside immediate political terms. Historians of this orientation have a preference for grasping conflicts as they arose, and as recorded in archival sources, setting aside the immediate strategic concerns of contemporary movements (to a greater or lesser extent).

This brings us to Jules Gill-Peterson's *Histories of the Transgender Child* (2018) and Christopher Chitty's *Sexual Hegemony* (2020). In each case, these books benefit from a certain detachment that genealogy's influence has afforded today's queer(?) history.

We find in Christopher Chitty's *Sexual Hegemony* a steadfast focus on 'sodomites', a moral term that became integrated into juridical statute and structure by early modernity. For instance, the Florentine police grandly titled the 'Office of the Night' was established with the suppression of sodomy as one of its primary concerns.

While some of the urban forms-of-life Chitty helps uncover may seem familiar to contemporary readers, in others he is unflinching in identifying the power mismatches which these varieties of homosexual relationship existed between. The political ramifications of bracketing together convicts from earlier modernity with legislation that has been repealed within living memory (and, in much of the former British Empire, remains in full force) are set to one side by *Sexual Hegemony*. Rather than hoping to provide direct utility to emancipatory movements, Chitty's agenda is grasping the tenuous integration which 'sodomites' as class actors seem to have deployed across time.

To put it another way, if John Boswell traced the unlikely history of pre-modern tolerance, Chitty's approach provides precisely the opposite: a historical materialist account of why exactly 'moral panics' that led to the persecution of 'sodomites' occurred when they did. In short, what Chitty offers is an analysis of the situation of state suppression in the context of political economy.

The genealogical mode attempts to shelve the utility of history as a guide to who *we* are, in favour of a closer focus on continuity of a different kind: rather than reconstructing a continuous *people*, it places the attention on the governing institutions (from states to professional bodies) which have made the oversight of sexuality simply one concern within a broader remit to tacitly dominate their subjects' behaviour.

From this point of view, identity distinctions which have since been firmed up may disappear, as their origin point comes into better view. In *Histories of the Transgender Child*, Jules Gill-Peterson shows us how one intersex variation, Congenital Adrenal Hypoplasia (CAH), came to have broader ramifications not only for quite distinct intersex variations, but children attempting transition. While the medical profession has recently taken measures to relocate CAH outside of intersex variations proper, in the course of the twentieth century these variations coming to be fully understood disrupted earlier protocols for sorting male from female.

In Gill-Peterson's account, physicians' attempts to come to terms with the conceptual pressure that the identification of CAH placed onto their clinical practice resulted in rearguard definitions and redefinitions relating to (perceived) gender deviance more generally. Rather than becoming more easily and analytically separable, intersex and trans children became shrouded in the same shadow.

Unlike Chitty's work, Gill-Peterson's monograph does attempt to verify the prior existence of a population now continuously cast as a novelty (transgender children). However, her primary concern is identifying an overarching governing principle developed by post-war sexuality: 'the racialising plasticity of gender'.

In a move that might surprise or even alarm many of today's US progressives, Gill-Peterson seems unsatisfied with an account of 'gender' which extends only from 1990 to the present, instead returning to the work of New Zealander sexologist John Money (whom she presents as coining the term while fully immersed in the racial hierarchies of the post–War United States, where Money had moved as a white migrant in 1947.)

Clearly, this account is not one designed to be 'useful' in the immediate sense for contemporary political struggles, given today's anti-trans voices are prone to referring to themselves as 'gender critical'. Yet nevertheless, this approach provides a more thorough account of the efforts early gender clinics undertook to sustain an increasingly fragile order. If nothing else, Gill-Peterson's *Histories* shows how empty any emancipatory hopes centred around timely access to physicians will be.

Between 'ethnicising' and unveiling, what mode of history seems likely to prevail in the coming years? Surely both.

Across the course of the whole of their careers as intellectuals, some *ad hoc* equivocation between each historical register outlined here should be expected. The 'popular history of homosexuality' is assured some place in emancipatory writing for as long as efforts continue to dehumanise LGBT people, or depict us as an unfortunate expression of novel ideologies. Meanwhile, genealogically informed work will often be required precisely to temper the overly exuberant (or misleadingly straightforward) accounts of historical conflicts spun by radicals and liberals alike.

The role of historians will always be methodologically heterogenous – given the diverse range of forms historical sources take and the variety of pressing concerns in play. But a certain attachment to awkward details seems to appear in a range of guises. Moment by moment, differing registers may be required in response to the deviants of bygone eras being either smoothed into our own understandings, or effaced from the record altogether.

CHINA MIÉVILLE

Communism, the *Manifesto*, and Hate

We have no reason to succumb to the complex comfort of despair, a lugubriousness by which failure is foreordained*. But to stress the repeated failures of the Left is a necessary corrective to its history of boosterism and bullshit, and to stress how appalling these days are, even if we can also find in them hope. To take the liberal approach and see Johnson, Bolsonaro, Modi, Duterte, the recently defenestrated Trump, Berlusconi and his aftermaths, violent and intricate 'conspiracism', the rise of the alt-right, the volubility of racism and fascism as *deviations* exonerates the system of which they are expressions. Trump is gone, but Trumpism remains strong.

But for all this, and for the recent defeat and smearing of left movements in Britain and the US, a cause of profound depression and demoralisation on the left, it's important to keep stressing that this has also been a moment of unprecedented insurgency in American cities. History, and the present, are up for debate.

---

* This is an edited extract from a forthcoming book with the working title *A Spectre Haunting: On the Communist Manifesto* (Head of Zeus, 2022).

Capitalism cannot exist without relentless punishment of those who transgress its often petty and heartless prohibitions, and indeed of those the punishment of whom it deems functional to its survival, irrespective of their notional 'transgression'. It – increasingly – deploys not just bureaucratic repression but an invested, overt, supererogatory sadism. The claim, in David Garland's thirty-year-old book *Punishment and Modern Society*, that '"punitiveness", as such, has come to be a rather shameful sentiment during the twentieth century ... so that arguments ... tend to be couched in utilitarian terms' now reads as painfully naïve: it was only five years after those words were written that Alabama reintroduced the chain gang for inmates, for the first time in forty years. In Georgia, the 'Tier Step Down' prison program involves the deliberate malnourishment of prisoners, the denial of access to education – and the inability to flush toilets. In 2014, an Ohio judge ruled that, in the words of the state's Attorney General, 'You're not entitled to a pain-free execution' – and the man subsequently executed by experimental cocktail of drugs, Dennis McGuire, did indeed visibly experience intense pain. In response to the horror, one public commentator in Florida writes: 'Who says that cold-blooded killers have a right to be executed like a worn-out puppy being put down?'

The separation of families at the borders of the United States; the deliberate malnourishment of Palestinians in Gaza through blockade – 'putting them on a diet', per Israeli official Dov Weissglas; the erstwhile US President's encouraging the police to commit acts of brutality in 2017 ('Don't be too nice.'); the sale of hooded sweatshirts commemorating the slow death of black men like Eric Garner at police hands ('Breathe Easy: Don't break the law', and 'I CAN BREATHE'). There are countless such ghastly examples of the rehabilitation and celebration of cruelty, in the carceral sphere, in politics and culture. Certainly such spectacles are not new, but they have not always been so 'unabashed', as Philip Mirowski puts it in *Never Let a Serious Crisis Go to Waste*, 'made to seem so unexceptional' – and they are not only distraction but part of 'teaching techniques optimised to reinforce the neoliberal self'.

Such social sadisms have always been opposed and fought over, and officially disavowed – particularly 'at home', rather than aimed at subjects of colonial rule – by structures that depict themselves as rational and just, even merciful. That's changing. These are more and more openly sadistic and apocalyptic times – and not without some popular support. And nor is the Left, in its various virtue-signalling iterations, immune to the addictive pull of a related *Schwarmerei* – purulent, swarmlike sentiment, and authoritarian sentimentality, visible for example in certain online shitstorms, in-group anathematisation, moralistic bullying.

This is a system that thrives on and encourages such sadism, despair and disempowerment. Alongside which are thrown up species of authoritarian notional 'happiness', an obligatory drab 'enjoyment' of life, a ruthless insistence on cheerfulness, such as Barbara Ehrenreich describes in her book *Smile or Die*. Such mandatory positivity is not the opposite, but the co-constitutive other, of such miseries. This is the bullying of what Lauren Berlant calls 'cruel optimism', including on the Left: no judicious earned optimism but a browbeating insistence on the necessity of positive thinking, at the cost not only of emotional autonomy but the inevitable crash when the world fails to live up to such strictures.

In a social system of mass cruelty, which celebrates only such miserable, commodified and ultimately impoverishing 'pleasures', it's perfectly understandable that the Left should be eager to stress a different kind and depth of positive emotion, to find potential radical opposition in, and socially destabilising inflections of, joy, taken to be the opposite of sadism, say. To see in love a shattering, reconfiguring event, a key revolutionary motivation. After all, the ethics underpinning socialism, says Terry Eagleton in his wonderful *Why Marx Was Right*, resolve a contradiction of liberalism 'in which your freedom may flourish only at the expense of mine', '[o]nly through others can we finally come into our own', which 'means an enrichment of individual freedom, not a diminishing of it. It is hard to think of a finer ethics. On a personal level, it is known as love'. This sense, to love, of a certain political prefiguration, has inspired radicals for a century. In her seminal 'Make Way for Winged Eros', the great revolutionary Alexandra Kollontai described love as 'a profoundly social emotion', insisted that '[f]or a social system to be built on solidarity and cooperation it is essential that people should be capable of love', and encouraged education to that end. How can we not, to quote the title of a fascinating and provocative recent book by Richard Gilman-Opalsky, consider 'the communism of love'? Be drawn by its claim that '[w]hat is called "love" by the best thinkers who have approached the subject is the beating heart of communism'.

By all means let us take love seriously.

But we must take our enemies seriously too, and learn from them. In what is an epoch of great hate.

In 1989, Donald Trump suggested that 'maybe hate is what we need if we're going to get something done'. His hatred was, and remains, a vicious deployment of racist class spite: a demand for the judicial murder of the Central Park five, black teenagers falsely accused of rape. The concrete content of his hate is everything against which we should stand. But how best to counter hate? Is such hate as this itself not worthy of hatred? Trump is shrewd. If not his initial aim, his hate certainly got something done. Perhaps, negatively inspired, our own hate should get something else done, and urgently. Something very different. To hate such systemic hate.

The philosopher and Anglican priest Steven Shakespeare warns that a focus on hate as anything other than a force to be rejected is 'fraught', 'dangerous territory'. How could it be otherwise? Hatred, after all, is an emotion that can short-circuit thought and analysis, segue into violence, and not necessarily with any discrimination.

But, duly careful, Steven Shakespeare then attempts exactly the focus about which he warns, precisely to be 'more discriminatory about hate, where it comes from, where it should be directed, and how it gets captured for the purposes of others'. A key point he makes is that hatred 'which assumes no founding truth or harmony, but ... knows itself to be against the dominating other' is 'a constituent part of the singularity of every created being'.

The claim, then, in the face of human history, is that hatred, particularly that felt by the oppressed, is *inevitable*.

This isn't to say that it's inevitable that all people, even all oppressed people, will experience hate. It's to claim that, hate being neither contingent nor alien to the human soul, some will. That, particularly in the contexts of societies that pit people against each other individually and *en masse*, hate will certainly exist. People will hate. As many of us know personally.

Hate is part of humanity. There's no guarantee of the direction of such inevitable hate, of course. It can be internalised, into the deadening self-hatred that, under capitalism, is so widespread. So often so validated by the system itself. Who, ground down by capitalism, does not feel, in the closing words of Rae Armantrout's poem 'Hate', that '[t]he market hates you / even more / than you hate yourself'? It can be externalised, without any justice: it has often been turned against those who least deserve it. But, though it has become a cliché, Marx's favourite maxim is richly pertinent here: *Nihil humani a me alienum puto* – nothing human is alien to me. It's hardly productive to pathologise hate *per se*, not least when it's natural that it arises, let alone to make it cause for shame.

Sophie Lewis puts the point with customary trenchant clarity, in her exhilarating 'Hello to my Haters'.

> Hate is almost never talked about as appropriate, healthy, or necessary in liberal-democratic society. For conservatives, liberals, and socialists alike, hate itself is the thing to reject, uproot, defeat, and cast out of the soul. Yet anti-hate ideology doesn't seem to involve targeting its root causes and points of production, nor does it address the inevitability of or the demand – the need – for hate in a class society.

To raise this issue, not only of the existence of hatred but, for some at least, its potential rigorous necessity, is, to put it in Kenneth Surin's terms, what lies behind 'deploying a deliberate hate as a rational category'. Hate should never be trusted, nor treated as safe, nor celebrated for its own sake. But, inevitable, it should not be ignored. Nor is it automatically undeserved. Nor, perhaps, can we do without it, not if we are to remain human, in a hateful epoch that pathologises radical hate and encourages outrage fatigue.

Nor is careful hate necessarily an enemy of liberation. It might be its ally.

In 1837, membership of the radical left group of the great pre-Marxian socialist Auguste Blanqui, known as the 'Seasons', made such socially informed hate central. Standing against the degradation of the revolutionary tradition, for freedom, acolytes swore an oath: 'In the name of the Republic, I swear eternal hatred to all kings, aristocrats and all oppressors of humanity.' In 1889, the radical Australian poet Francis Adams wrote that he had destroyed his health in the pursuit of working-class struggle in London. 'It seemed a failure', he wrote. 'But I never despaired, or saw cause to despair. There was a splendid foundation of hate there. With hate, all things are possible.' In 1957, Dorothy Counts desegregated a school in North Carolina. Writing of the photograph of her walking past the vicious jeering mob of demonstrators, James Baldwin wrote that '[i]t made me furious. It filled me with both hatred and pity'. The latter for Counts; the former for what he saw in the faces of her attackers. It would be an astonishing and priggish piety to suggest that hatred such as this was unbecoming, or that it did not work for emancipation.

Crucially, as Francis Adams wrote, *all* things are possible with hate – not only good things. That's the danger. But some good things, surely, in terms, for example, of activist vigour. Raging, too, certainly, but raging *against* something, wishing its eradication. The very absence of a critical mass of hatred may militate against resistance: Walter Benjamin, in his extraordinary, prophetic, controversial 1940 essay 'Theses on the Philosophy of History', took social democracy, as opposed to militant socialism, to task for its focus on the future and on the working class as 'redeemer', thus actively weakening that class by directing its eyes away from the iniquities of the past, to 'forget both its hatred and its spirit of sacrifice'. It was in part in this hatred that he thought there might be strength.

And hate may help not only with strength but intellectual rigour. And with analysis too. The very flat abstractions of capital can generate their own seemingly implacable logic, against which an emotionally invested eye, a *hating* contrary eye, might prove necessary not only ethically but epistemologically. 'What will never function is the cold logic of reason', Mario Tronti writes in *Workers and Capital*, 'when it is not moved by class hatred.' Because 'knowledge is connected to the struggle. Whoever has true hatred has truly understood.' Tronti goes so far as to describe a radical antinomianism, that is, opposition to 'the entire world of bourgeois society, as well as deadly class hatred against it' as 'the simplest form of Marx's working class science'. Even in Marx's early political writings, from 1848–9, wrong as they were in various particulars, Tronti finds 'a clear-sightedness in foreseeing future development such as only class hatred could provide.'

Class hatred. Hatred by a social force, of an opposing social force, of that 'dominating other' Steven Shakespeare identifies. Such a hate is just, indicated and necessary: 'not a personal, psychological or pathological hate, but a radical structural hate for what the world has become'.

Such radical structural hate, carefully deployed, might even give productive shape to the more protean forms of hate that are also inevitable, and more dangerous. 'The proposed melding here of hate with a strategic logic', for Surin, 'is essential if hate is not to descend into rage or a mindless apocalypticism'. Hate will arise, and though shame should not attach to it, it must be urgently directed. '*Radical* hate', in Mike Neary's description, 'is the critical concept on which absolute negativity' – that antinomian rupture – 'is based'.

Even so subtle and hate-curious a Marxologist as Tronti focuses on and finds his material in Marx's writings other than *The Communist Manifesto*. But those texts precisely come after the *Manifesto*, and can be seen in part as responses to it and to its failures, the failures of its prophecies, its hopes. The class hatred those later writings express doesn't emerge out of nowhere.

In the rhetoric of the *Manifesto* itself, Haig Bosmajian sees 'not only attempts to arouse anger … but … to arouse hatred which is directed not only against an individual, but also against a class'. He quotes Aristotle in suggesting that where anger provokes a desire for revenge, '"hatred wishes its object not to exist"', and that Marx's 'goal was to arouse his listeners to that state in which they would wish the bourgeoisie eradicated'. This is ambiguous: the point for Marx and Engels isn't the 'eradication' of individuals, but of the bourgeoisie *as a class* – which is to say, of capitalism. To suggest that the text evokes 'hatred' of bourgeois individuals is to misrepresent the ambivalence in its passages, as well as its focus on the class system of capitalism. To go further and claim, as does Leo Kuper, that the 'thoroughgoing dehumanization of the bourgeoisie' has 'relevance' for the problem of *genocide*, implying a teleology of 'the inevitable violent extinction of a dehumanized class of people' is absurd.

On the one hand, this is simply to deploy the question-begging liberal nostrum that Stalin is the inevitable outcome and end of Marxism, and is thus not particularly interesting or surprising. It should of course be acknowledged that there are those who have used such arguments as are in the *Manifesto* to commit appalling acts. Still, though, describing this imaginary terror sententiously as one meted out on the basis of guilt ascribed to people 'for what they are, rather than for what they do', in one commentator's words, is precisely wrong. In the *Manifesto*, in Marxism in general, the relation between classes is definitionally not on the basis of static, given identities, but relations, which include things done. And the 'eradication' necessary is of those relations, not of specific people. The *Manifesto* is clear: 'To be a capitalist is to have not only a purely personal but a social position in production.' And not by essence of self, either, as the *Manifesto*'s description of class renegacy among some of the bourgeoisie attests, but by virtue of actively perpetuating structures and dynamics of capital accumulation, taking positions reflecting such a tendency – and that of concomitant immiseration and disempowerment. It's precisely the pressing need for rupture in the *Manifesto* that expresses what radical hatred it contains.

But in any case, in fact, for all their magnificent spleen against the system, Marx and Engels were too generous in their eulogy to its transformation and energetic properties, and to the bourgeoisie itself – as well as about the likelihood of its collapse. The *Manifesto* is a call to arms, but those real traces of a sense of inevitable col-lapse pull against that drive to *eradicate* the system. The *Manifesto* hopes to be a swan song of the system, but it is, too, a certain kind of hymn to its glory.

> Never, I repeat, and in particular by no modern defender of the bourgeois civilization has anything like this been penned, never has a brief been composed on behalf of the business class from so profound and so wide a comprehension of what its achievement is and of what it means to humanity.

If this, from the conservative economist Joseph Schumpeter, is an exaggeration, it isn't by much.

The *Manifesto*, for all its fire, its anger and indignation, admires capitalism and bourgeois society and the bourgeoisie. It admires the bourgeois class too much.

It's telling that Gareth Stedman Jones, a relentlessly disillu-sioned biographer of Marx, describes the tone of the *Manifesto*'s most well-known passage as one of 'playful sadism'. One might well contest the noun, but not the adjective. And to be playful, to play, implies a playmate. The very scintillation and swaggering provoca-tion that makes the *Manifesto* so brilliant implies, for all its antago-nism, something ludic, that pulls against any eliminationist hatred in the text.

This is not to imply that the *Manifesto* is hate-free. It admires the bourgeoisie, plays roughly with them, and hates them too, no doubt. Of course hatred of the system is clear throughout. But at its most combative, how hard does it hate the bourgeoisie as a class? In the most antagonistic section, the bourgeoisie are argued with directly. That switch to second person locates what hatred there is in, or at least inextricable from, the admiration. They are lazy, the text insists ('bourgeois society ought long ago to have gone to the dogs through sheer idleness'); and selfish ('The selfish misconcep-tion that induces you to transform into eternal laws of nature and of reason, the social forms springing from your present mode of production and form of property'), and hypocritical ('bourgeois clap-trap about the family and education, about the hallowed co-relation of parents and child' is 'disgusting'). These are about all, as far as direct attacks go. And the sincere fury here sits atop that play, the enjoyment of winning an argument, rhetorical roughhousing. But is the direct scorn here greater than in the ferocious attacks on various left opponents? If anything, the palpable vituperation against, say, the True Socialists, is greater, precisely because it has none of that ambivalence in attitude that the *Manifesto* has towards the bourgeoisie.

To borrow a phrase from Neary, in another context, *The Communist Manifesto*'s 'negativity is not negative enough'. It does not hate enough. Against the rolling eyes of the know-all cynic, we should retain shock at those litanies of iniquity capitalism throws up. That they provoke in us an appropriate, human, humane response, the fury of solidarity, the loathing of such unnecessary suffering. Who would we be not to hate this system, and its partisans? If we don't, the hate of those who hate on its behalf will not ebb. '[T]here's a splendid foundation of hate today, too', Jeff Sparrow shrewdly warns '– and if we don't build something positive from it, the edifices that will inevitably emerge will be very ugly indeed.' We should feel hate beyond words, and bring it to bear. This is a system that deserves implacable hatred for its countless and escalating cruelties.

The ruling class needs the working class. Its various fantasies of eradicating them, of a world of gated communities without the rebuke of their presence, can only *be* fantasies, because as a class it has no power without those beneath it. Thus wider ruling-class contempt for the working class ('chavs'), thus class loathing, thus social sadism, thus the constant entitlement from the ruling class, that sense that they are special and that rules don't apply, thus the deranged eulogising of cruelty and inequality. Vile as all this is, what it is not is *hate*, certainly not Aristotelian hate – because its object absolutely cannot be eradicated.

For the working class, the situation is different. The eradication of the bourgeoisie *as a class* is the eradication of bourgeois rule, of capitalism, of exploitation, of the boot on the neck of humanity. This is why the working class doesn't need sadism, nor even revenge – and why it not only can, but must, hate. It must hate its class enemy, and capitalism itself.

There is a model for a better hatred in one of the key texts from which the *Manifesto* was born, Engels' *The Conditions of the Working Class in England*. Hate, of the most class-rigorous kind, recurs and recurs repeatedly, runs through that unendingly shocked and blistering work. It recognises in the bourgeoisie, for its part, 'hatred towards these associations' of the working class, of course. Those *associations* the bourgeoisie could certainly do with eradicating. But not only does Engels not shy from the hate of the working class for its oppressors, in turn, but he repeatedly invokes it, and more.

He sees it as necessary and central to working-class politics. Workers, for Engels, 'shall live like human beings, shall think and feel like men [sic]' 'only under glowing hatred towards their oppressors, and towards that order of things which places them in such a position, which degrades them to machines'. Hatred is necessary for dignity, which means for political agency. He doesn't celebrate hate *tout court*, all too aware of the dangers of 'hatred wrought to the pitch of despair' and manifesting in individual attacks by workers on capitalists. 'Class hatred', by contrast, is 'the only moral incentive by which the worker can be brought nearer the goal.' This stands in direct opposition to individualised hatred: 'in proportion as the proletarian absorbs socialistic and communistic elements, will the revolution diminish in bloodshed, revenge, and savagery ... [I]t does not occur to any Communist to wish to revenge himself upon individuals'.

It would admittedly be a prim and pious socialism which failed at least to empathise with individualised hate, or simply denounced it wholesale as an ethical failure. This is particularly so in our modern epoch, when sadism and trolling have become central to political method, especially among the ruling class. It would take an unreasonable amount of saintliness for anyone on the left not to feel any hate for, say, hedge fund founder, pharmaceuticals CEO and convicted fraudster Martin Shkreli, for example, not only because of his ostentatious profiteering from human misery, but given his repeated, performative, stringent efforts to be hated. And of course there's the race-baiting, disability-mocking, sexual-assault-celebrating Trump.

The point, though, is that to fully and uncritically surrender to such agon against individuals is to invite one's own ethical degeneration; to implicitly give a pass to those others in the ruling class more inclined to decorously veil the misery from which they profit; and to lose focus on the system of which such turpitudinous figures are symptoms. Which is to risk exonerating it.

The history of the revolutionary movement is, among other things, a history of organised radicals attempting to *restrain* individualised class hate – think of Antonov defending the members of the Provisional Government from the murderous anger of Red Guards in 1917. Hatred must be *class* hatred, with 'communistic ideas', precisely to obviate 'the present bitterness'. But that class hate is glowing and must glow, and only by 'cherishing' it can those at the sharp end of history keep self-respect alive. Herein lies the 'purity' of which the radical journalist Alexander Cockburn enquired when he famously asked of his interns, 'Is your hate pure?' This is a political iteration of the הָאֲנֹשׁ תִּילַכַת, the *taklit sinah*, the 'utmost' or 'perfect hatred' of the Psalms for those who rise up against the Lord – that is to say, to translate into political eschatology, the enemies of justice. Psalm 139.22: 'I hate them with a perfect hatred.'

We must hate harder than did the *Manifesto*, for the sake of humanity. Such class hate is constitutive with and inextricable from solidarity, the drive for human liberty, for the full development of the human, the ethic of emancipation implicit throughout the *Manifesto* and beyond. We should hate this world, with and through and beyond and even more than does the *Manifesto*. We should hate this hateful and hating and hatemongering system of cruelty, that exhausts and withers and kills us, that stunts our care, makes it so embattled and constrained and local in its scale and effects, where we have the capacity to be greater.

Hate is not and cannot be the only or main drive to renewal. That would be deeply dangerous. We should neither celebrate nor trust our hate. But nor should we deny it. It's not our enemy, and we cannot do without it. 'At the risk of seeming ridiculous', said Che Guevara, 'let me say that the true revolutionary is guided by a great feeling of love.' It's for the sake of love that, reading it today, we must hate more and better than even *The Communist Manifesto* knew how.

HEBA HAYEK

Special Plants

After multiple visits to see the doctor and a range of blood tests, we found out that my grandmother had been high for most of 2012*.

On joyful occasions, she would sit in front of a forty-quart stock pot to make sumagiyya, the quintessential flour and sumac infusion dish known exclusively to Gazans and only served during celebrations, never funerals or sad days. Sitti would make za'atar and fresh red chilli paste for dozens of households, and we'd all eat her food in bliss. When she got a bit older, she started making her own bread and only ate fresh produce, including her special home-grown health plants. She had a plant for every possible complication a woman of her age could have, completely convinced that she was not supposed to age.

Until she discovered Google and began voraciously reading random tips online, Sitti was incredible at giving nutritional advice. She had given birth to thirteen children, and it was rumoured that some of my uncles and aunties grew teeth at six months because of how healthy her milk was. She took pride in her knowledge, and

* With thanks to Hajar Press for their permission to publish extracts from *Sambac Beneath Unlikely Skies*.

169

many women visited her house to leave with blessings and recipes they swore by.

When military escalations were carried out by the occupation forces, or anything bad happened to us, Sitti was excellent at physical therapy. All children would go to her house so that she could relieve our muscle knots. We called it 'cutting the fear'. She would massage our bodies with olive oil wherever tension might reside, reading Al-Mu'awwidhat, the three protective suras in the Qur'an.

I seek refuge with the Lord from every evil and mischief of every creature. (114)

Some children would get ticklish, and she would laugh with them; others would cry from pain and she would soothe them.

Sitti's voice was soft. She compensated for that with a filthy mouth, which was passed down to the other women of the family when they reached an appropriate age. We all had it in us. She was born a year before the Nakba and was carried by her parents from her village in Jaffa to Gaza in 1948. On the long way to the refugee camp, she lost her father. She grew up in a tent with seven siblings, of whom only two were alive when I was born. No one remembered the date when she was born, so we assumed her birthday based on her personality: only on days when it rained heavily in December did we celebrate Sitti's birth, for in her hands she had khair and blessings like ripe fruits.

In her living room was a sofa with a butt-shaped impression where she sat for most of the day when she wasn't in the mosque studying Qur'an. She wasn't a big fan of visiting people in their homes, and when she did, she would always criticise something or other and would never touch the food. Whenever she visited us, she'd find dust on top of the fridge and denigrate Mama's standards of cleanliness, so we'd just go to her house to avoid having her over.

I sat on the floor while she massaged my hair with some seed oil she was growing.

'Is this why you didn't visit me last week? You were hiding it.'

I knew she hated it when I cut my hair. All of my cousins who lived in her house had long beautiful hair, but Mama let me cut mine whenever I wanted. It was supposed to make it grow faster, but it never ended up growing enough, because I always cut it before it had the chance.

'Mama said I could cut it.' I threw my mother under the bus.

'Ye'ta'a Israel.' *May God cut Israel*, she said casually. 'You know the reason why your sido married me was because of my hair? It was so thick and long that I couldn't close my grip around it.'

I looked at her squeezing oil into her palms and thought, *that's not so thick*. And it wasn't like she had been happy with my grandpa; they had argued like the sun and the moon. When Sido passed away, Sitti seemed like she'd gained back ten years of her life—even though he was easy to get along with, and we all preferred him to her. Sido was kind and sweet, until they were in each other's company. Even so, she went on and on about how thin and pretty and young she had been then, and how crazy about her he was.

Outside, it was hailing for the first time in years. Mama and I had come to visit Sitti because she was feeling sick, and to entertain her on her alleged birthday. Maybe we'd even bake something she wouldn't eat.

'How old are you now, Sitti?'

'Fifty.'

'You were sixty last year.'

Her shoulders moved up and down in rhythmic approval and contentment.

'Well then, fifteen.'

'That sounds accurate.'

That day, we finally convinced her to go to the doctor's because she was feeling dizzy and tired. It turned out that abundantly consuming moringa and morning glory seeds was making her high on psychedelics, and wonderfully young as well. The red ginseng, meanwhile, was making her horny.

At London Stansted Airport, I stamp my passport after finally managing to get a Schengen visa to visit my brother in Düsseldorf. My mother makes us promise to go and visit our grandma in Wavre, a two-hour drive away in Belgium. After many denied permits to seek further medical help for her arthritis, Sitti's pain had become unbearable, and Western medicine had seemed like the final choice. I haven't spoken to her in four years, and she hasn't been very happy with most of my decisions since I left Gaza. But she arrived in Europe only recently to seek asylum with two of my uncles, and it's only appropriate that we pay her a visit.

I clip in my very cheap hair extensions, which I ordered especially for this trip. My hair has only grown down to my ears since I last cut it, and I can't risk it.

We park our car and ring the bell at the only building on the green, sandy road. We are greeted with excessive love and hugs by our uncle's family. Sitti is sitting on a bed in the corner of the living room, reading the Qur'an, which she puts away with her reading glasses as we enter.

We are never prepared for moments like these. Seventy years since her birth, our grandma is in a French-speaking town, barely able to move, again a refugee. She tells me that she didn't want to leave Gaza, and that she regrets it.

'Who leaves at this age?' she says, slightly ashamed of her attempt at survival. As though there were an age limit to craving life, or to that quiet longing older folks back home often fear expressing.

My extensions don't succeed in hiding the mischief I've been up to over the years I've spent away from her. I sit on the floor in a two-bedroom council house where thirteen people live, guilty about my own efforts at survival.

'Was this really the best you could do?' she laughs. 'If I were you, I'd start by calling Sitti more often. Now, come sit here and let me try this hair oil I've just bought from Carrefour.'

About the Contributors

LUÍSA CALVETE PORTELA BARBOSA is an academic from Brazil now based in London. She is a Lecturer of International Relations at Cardiff University and a volunteer at LAWRS, where she is working on a report about the work and life conditions of Latin American domestic workers in Britain.

TAD DELAY PhD teaches philosophy in Baltimore. He is currently writing his fourth book, Denial Futures.

JULES JOANNE GLEESON is a writer, comedian and salonnière from London, based in Vienna. She co-edited *Transgender Marxism*, and her own essays have been widely published. Her performances have included lectures delivered at festivals and retreats worldwide, and stand-up sets for Vienna's Activist Comedy Against Bullshit, and Politically Correct Comedy Club. She's currently working on a book about hermaphrodites, sexual indifference, and inferentialist logic.

HEBA HAYEK is a London-based writer born and raised in Gaza, Palestine. She completed an MFA in Creative Writing at Miami University, Ohio, and is studying for an MA in Social Anthropology at SOAS University of London, where she is working on an autoethnography about Gazan women in the US and Britain. Heba has been involved in several activist movements, including for BDS, prison abolition and demilitarisation. *Sambac Beneath Unlikely Skies* is her first book, published by Hajar Press.

SARAH JAFFE is the author of *Work Won't Love You Back: How Devotion to Our Jobs Keeps Us Exploited, Exhausted and Alone* and of *Necessary Trouble: Americans in Revolt.* She is a Type Media Center reporting fellow and an independent journalist covering the politics of power, from the workplace to the streets. Her work has appeared in the *New York Times*, the *Nation*, the *Guardian*, the *Washington Post*, the *New Republic*, the *Atlantic*, and many other publications. She is the co-host, with Michelle Chen, of *Dissent* magazine's Belabored podcast, as well as a columnist at the *Progressive* and *New Labor Forum*.

CHINA MIÉVILLE is a founding editor of *Salvage*. He is the author of various works of fiction and non-fiction, including *This Census-Taker* and *October: The Story of the Russian Revolution*.

KEVIN OCHIENG OKOTH is a writer and researcher living in London. He is a corresponding editor at *Salvage*.

PATTY PAINE is the author of *Grief & Other Animals*, *The Sounding Machine*, and three chapbooks. She edited *Gathering the Tide: An Anthology of Contemporary Arabian Gulf Poetry* and *The Donkey Lady and Other Tales from the Arabian Gulf*. Her poems and artwork have appeared in *Blackbird*, *Adroit*, *Gulf Stream*, *Waxwing*, *Thrush*, *The South Dakota Review*, and other publications. She is the founding editor of *Diode Poetry Journal*, and Diode Editions, and is Director of Liberal Arts & Sciences at VCUarts Qatar.

BARNABY RAINE studies social and political thought at Columbia University, where he is writing his PhD on the decline of visions of ending capitalism.

RICHARD SEYMOUR is an author, and a founding editor of *Salvage*. His most recent book is *The Twittering Machine*.